THE
BLK
TUX

The Groom's Guide

FOR MEN ON THE VERGE OF MARRIAGE

DOVETAIL

Ignore anyone who tells you there are rules you must follow.

Contents

Welcome to Groomdom

I

Dearly beloved, we are gathered here today to figure out this whole wedding thing. From the food, florist, and first dance song, to where to seat your handsy great aunt at the reception— it's hard to fathom just how many decisions are involved in planning a wedding until you're neck-deep in them. Then, one day, you wake up in a cold sweat from a nightmare about your tuxedo pants making it look like someone "Honey I Shrunk" you.

There's no single emotion that describes wedding planning: It's overwhelming but fun and exciting at the same time. Simply put, *it's complicated.*

But before you decide to throw in the towel on this whole complicated wedding thing, book it to Vegas, and let Elvis marry you, let us reassure you: We get it. We're here for you. And we're going to get through this together.

What you have in your sweaty palms is a guidebook for discovering what you want out of the wedding experience. We'll cover things like picking your suit and guest list, how to make a toast, and whether you should have an open bar at your reception (that's actually not even a question). Unlike your family and all those judgy wedding message boards online (tip #1: stay away from the message boards), this guide will never tell you that there's one right way to do a wedding. It also won't push a single viewpoint on heavy subjects like money, religion, politics, or family drama. We much prefer to focus on the fun stuff—what's so wrong with that?

What we will do is give you our best ideas for creating an ass-kicking wedding experience, whatever that means for you. Think of this guide as one big "getting married" Pinterest board, but without the DIY glitter-and-popsicle-sticks stuff. In fact, the only appearance popsicle sticks make in this book will be when we advocate for serving corn dogs as midnight snacks at the reception. If that sounds like something you're into, then read on, because this is going to be the beginning of a beautiful friendship—one that hopefully involves a lot of fried food.

Good luck!

If you need further advice beyond what's in this guide, don't hesitate to drop us a line at support@theblacktux.com. We'll never leave you hanging.

Groom forth and prosper.

HOW TO READ THIS BOOK

PIECE OF CAKE
TIME TO SAY "THANK YOU"

should be sent out within three months
...y, to everyone who touched your wedding
wedding party, the guests, even the ven-
l be hand written and personalized. If you
onth mark, remember: Better late than
ank-you notes a year after the wedding is
...ss so than no thank-you note at all.

PIECE OF CAKE ↗

Think of these as pro tips:
simple ways to make your time as
a fiancé less complicated. With
these easy suggestions, you'll
save time, money, your sanity, or
maybe even all of the above.

ILLUSTRATIONS →

Because we're all adults here, we all know
that adults secretly wish their books had
more pictures. Well, we have no shortage
of them in ours. Some of the pictures are
instructional (like a diagram of how to
tie a bow tie), while some of them are
a piece of toast wearing a veil (wedding
toast... get it? We crack ourselves up).

CHECKLIST ↙

What do you need to accomplish
on the day of your wedding? What
do you pack for your honeymoon?
It can be easy to forget amidst
the stress of planning, so we
lay it out for you. Feel free to
actually fill in the boxes.

CHECKLIST	
Eat breakfast	
Kill the rehearsal-dinner hangover (if you pac... don't have one, congratulations—we're not all ...	
Review your schedule for the day	
Make sure you're packed for your honeymoon	
Write out a list of people you need to talk to/thank/dance with at the reception	
Double check with the best man that he has the rings	

FOLIOS →

This book was made to be marked up, dog-eared, and returned to for quick reference later. These little tabs letting you know which section you're in put the "quick" in quick reference, making it easy for you to look up stuff on a whim.

PHOTOS ↖

There are a lot of nice photos of weddings in this guide. We hope they'll inspire you and get you excited about your own big day. There are also a lot of educational photos. They'll teach you about things like how a suit should fit, and which one is right for your style and dress code.

Groom Service

TAKE A TIMEOUT FOR TWO

easy to get caught up in the excitement of the party, but be sure steal a moment alone with your partner sometime during or ht after the reception. It's important for the two of you to revel he utter coolness of what you just did—you're a married couple now! Bring on the new life phase.

GROOM SERVICE →

These are the non-negotiables of being a groom. Follow these tips and you might just win the "Groom of the Year" award (if it actually existed). Ignore them at your peril.

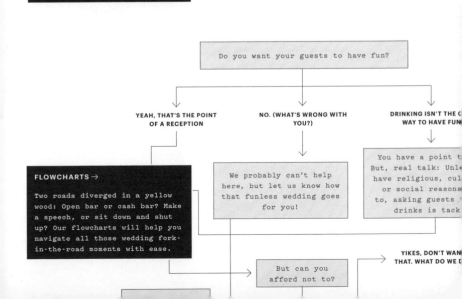

Do you want your guests to have fun?

YEAH, THAT'S THE POINT OF A RECEPTION

NO. (WHAT'S WRONG WITH YOU?)

DRINKING ISN'T THE (WAY TO HAVE FUN

FLOWCHARTS →

Two roads diverged in a yellow wood: Open bar or cash bar? Make a speech, or sit down and shut up? Our flowcharts will help you navigate all those wedding fork-in-the-road moments with ease.

We probably can't help here, but let us know how that funless wedding goes for you!

You have a point t But, real talk: Unl have religious, cul or social reasons to, asking guests drinks is tack

But can you afford not to?

YIKES, DON'T WAN THAT. WHAT DO WE [

The 10-Minute Cheat Sheet

II

Books aren't for everyone—just ask any Hollywood studio executive. That's why we're giving you the literary equivalent of the carpool lane. You'll miss out on the wit, humor, and insight that reading this entire guide offers (plus there's free money hidden within), but on the flip-side, you'll have way more time for push-ups. You're getting into wedding shape, right?

General Planning

DO (AT LEAST) THESE 10 THINGS

→ Find and book an officiant, DJ/band, caterer, baker, florist, and photographer

→ Make a guest list and seating chart

→ Register for gifts

→ Reserve hotel rooms for your wedding night, and for guests

→ Rent your tuxedo or suit, and choose groomsmen attire

→ Buy your partner a gift, pick up wedding rings, and get groomsmen gifts

→ Attend and survive your bachelor party

→ Book and pack for honeymoon

→ Write your vows and a toast for the reception

→ Get a haircut and try on your suit

GUEST LISTS SUCK—DO THIS

Stand your ground. Make a list that ensures you'll be able to visually identify every guest, *and* be happy to see them.

THE 3 BIGGEST QUESTIONS TO ASK ANY VENDOR

→ How many weddings have you done?

→ How do deposits and payments work?

→ What happens if you are sick or unable to work the day of my wedding?

Ceremony

DON'T BRING YOUR PHONE

Live in the moment and let your guests, and your expensive photographer, take photos.

ON CHOOSING AN OFFICIANT

Choose a legally qualified, eloquent, entertaining person with whom you connect—and, if desired, who represents your chosen religion.

CHOOSE YOUR BEST MAN AND GROOMSMEN

Narrow your selection to five guys who have been like brothers, if not your actual brothers. Come to think of it, include your brothers if you have any. Be sure your best man is trustworthy and responsible—he's got a lot to handle.

HAVE AN OPINION

If you don't want to use your own ideas and opinions to help plan, someone else will make those decisions for you. The result? Often, regret and disappointment.

ON CHOOSING A MEANINGFUL SYMBOLIC ACT

There's nothing wrong with the classics, but consider whether the act you choose is actually meaningful or unique to you and your partner.

THE BEST USE OF WEDDING PHOTOS

Frame them! This solves the "out of sight, out of mind" problem of the wedding album.

Reception

CHOOSE YOUR DINNER

→ Sit-Down: The most formal and often the most expensive option.

→ Family-Style: Fosters a feeling of togetherness, with lower formality.

→ Buffet: Medium formality, medium price, medium chance you'll run out.

→ Food Truck: This is not your grandpa's wedding. Unless he loves tacos.

ON THE GROOM'S CAKE

If it doesn't look like an advertisement, you're doing it right.

LATE NIGHT MUNCHIES

Plan a snack that will keep your guests (safely) drinking and (recklessly) dancing.

ON THE QUESTION OF DRINKS

What do you mean, "question"? An open bar is the only answer.

ON THE QUESTION OF MUSIC

A live band brings the experience to you. A DJ allows you and your guests to create the experience. Choose your destiny.

CHOOSE A FIRST DANCE SONG

Ideally, the song will have special meaning between you and your partner, be event appropriate, and avoid clichés.

THE PERFECT MUSIC MIX

Keep them dancing, and occasionally moon walking, to songs they know and love.
No Macarena.

GET THE MOST OUT OF YOUR RSVP CARDS

Ask guests to draw a picture of you and your partner on the back of the RSVP card, and display them in a gallery at the reception.

Crowd-source your playlist by asking that music requests be noted on the RSVP.

Request guests provide a little-known fact about themselves on their RSVP, and use the responses to play wedding bingo at your reception, matching responses to corresponding guests.

Post-Reception & Beyond

YOUR AFTER-PARTY SHORTLIST

→ Karaoke bar

→ Classic greasy-spoon diner

→ Alcohol-friendly arcade

ON THE QUESTION OF HONEYMOON TIMING

Don't go back to real life just yet: Delaying your honeymoon means leaving that surreal wedding bubble. Keep the magic alive.

ONE HONEYMOON OOO REPLY:

```
To: <All Office>
Subject: Automatic Reply: "OOO"
_____
Thanks for reaching out! While you're
at it, could you reach out to my
lower back? I definitely didn't get
sunscreen there. Thanks—resuming
honeymoon now.
```

Read on
to achieve
nuptial
nirvana.

The
Big Picture

"Logistics" is such a boring word. We prefer to call them "party foundations."

1

So, You're Getting Married

You got down on one knee. Or you hid the ring in a slice of cake (why?). Or maybe you were just sitting on the couch watching a movie and eating chips, when you turned to your partner and said, "Hey, we should get married." However you did it, you're deep in it now. You have to plan a wedding, and—warning—it's not going to be easy. But we'll make it a little easier.

In this section, we'll wade through the logistics: finding the right vendors, building a seating chart that doesn't result in daytime soaps-level drama, and generally maintaining your precious sanity in the months and weeks leading up to the wedding day. (This last one may be hard at times, but you can do it.) The cake-tasting, band-booking, and honeymoon planning starts now.

DON'T SWEAT THE SMALL STUFF

WHEN PLANNING A WEDDING, it's easy to get sucked into a black hole of florists or place-setting options. Truth is, your guests probably aren't going to care much about that stuff. To avoid wedding burnout, invest your time and budget in the things they will remember (and gossip about).

Here's a handy diagram to help you figure out where to put your energy.

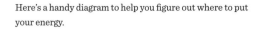

INDULGENT

TRANSCENDENT LOVE-FEST
Paul McCartney plays
original composition written
for the couple. Newlyweds
ride tigers into
the sunset.

B.W.O.A.T. (BEST WEDDING OF ALL TIME)
Fireworks display concludes ceremony.
Cups runneth over with sweet nectar,
band with horn section, grandpa drops
it low, religious officiant grinding with
weird aunt.

ONE FOR THE RECORD BOOKS
Gondola ferries bride and groom to
reception. Conga line or limbo is likely,
champagne pyramid attempted, catering servers
have spontaneous crowd circle dance battle.

A MEMORABLE AFFAIR
Surprise reading from a sibling, weeping occurs. Fully open
bar, cake of multiple tiers, catering from a Food Network
notable, the married couple ballroom dance to applause.

WEDDING FUNDAMENTALS
Brief ceremony in which marriage occurs. Guests consume enough
calories to stay awake, potable drinks that don't run out, music
sufficiently amplified.

SIMPLE

REMEMBER

The more selfies you're taking, the less you're enjoying your wedding.

Live in the moment, and leave the documenting to your photographer and guests.

A NOTE ON HAVING AN OPINION

SAYING "I DON'T CARE" won't get you anywhere. Remember, this is your day too! If you don't speak up, other people will make the big decisions for you. That means you may end up feeling uncomfortable in a weird tuxedo, eating food you hate at a table with ugly place settings, or—worst of all—having to do a choreographed dance with your partner. It's fine if you don't know exactly what you want for every detail of your wedding (that's what wedding planners are for!), but you should at least have a few general ideas and opinions about what you like and don't like—then leave the rest to the experts.

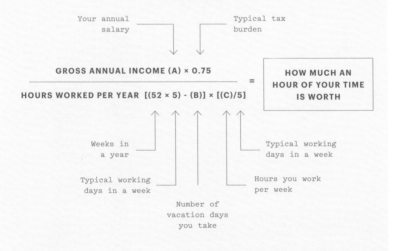

Time Is Money

This equation can you help you figure out if doing it yourself is actually more cost-effective than outsourcing to an expert, no matter what the wedding task.

Your annual salary → Typical tax burden

$$\frac{\text{GROSS ANNUAL INCOME (A)} \times 0.75}{\text{HOURS WORKED PER YEAR } [(52 \times 5) - (B)] \times [(C)/5]} = \boxed{\text{HOW MUCH AN HOUR OF YOUR TIME IS WORTH}}$$

Weeks in a year · Typical working days in a week · Typical working days in a week · Hours you work per week · Number of vacation days you take

- If you don't have a lot of disposable income, your time "value" goes down because you are better served saving money
- • If you have less free time, the value of each hour increases.

Before the Wedding

2

Truth: Weddings are 91 percent planning, 9 percent enjoying the fruits of your labor. Months and months of tastings, bookings, fittings, other people's opinions, petty arguments and (thankfully) even a little fun go into preparing for this one day. But it's all worth it in the end, because your wedding will be one of the best days of your life. These are our best tips and tools for getting through the 91 percent, and making sure the 9 percent makes everything else seem worth it.

"Sanity and happiness are an impossible combination."

—MARK TWAIN

HOW TO CHOOSE YOUR BEST MAN AND GROOMSMEN

CHOOSING YOUR BEST MAN and groomsmen is probably the biggest decision you'll have to make in the wedding planning process. Your selection should represent your A-team, your brotherhood... and your partner's younger brother who you've met twice. That being said, it can be hard to narrow down your friend group to the appropriate number of groomsmen (no more than five, in our opinion), and choose who should be your best man. Here are a few questions to ask yourself as you make your choices.

Who's Your Best Man, Man?

GET THE "HAVE TO" GUYS OUT OF THE WAY FIRST:
→ Do you have any brothers?
→ Does your partner have any brothers?
→ Any age-appropriate brothers should be included in the wedding party in some way.

EASIEST WAY TO CHOOSE YOUR BEST MAN:
→ Who is your oldest, closest friend?

ALSO:
→ Who can you trust with things like planning the bachelor party, and—most importantly—not losing the rings?

How to Identify the Groomsmen in Your Life

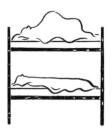

Who was your first roommate?

Who helped you get through the most difficult time in your life?

Who is at the center of your craziest travel story?

Who was there the first time you threw up from alcohol?

Who knew you during your awkward "pimples and pokémon" phase?

Who are your other closest childhood friends?

PIECE OF CAKE
NARROW YOUR GROOMSMEN LIST

Normally we wouldn't advocate ranking people, but this is a special case. It's time to rank your friends. Anyone beyond position #5 should be made an usher or cut (survival of the fittest, man). After you've successfully cut down your list, congratulate yourself: you've got yourself a wedding party.

THE ART OF THE GUEST LIST

THE SECRET TO BUILDING the perfect guest list is to stand your ground. Maybe you and your partner want a small, intimate wedding, but your families are pressuring you to invite every third cousin twice removed. Or maybe you want a big, blowout, party-of-the-century reception, but the peanut gallery is telling you to keep your guest list short.

Here's the thing: It's not their wedding.

Memorize this line. Repeat it to yourself often. This is your mantra, and it will help you get through more than just planning your guest list—it'll help you get through the entire wedding process.*

That being said, there is an art to crafting a guest list that involves assembling the perfect mix of people. The ratio of friends to family should be about even (or slightly favor friends, if possible), or the party may feel more like it belongs to your parents than you and your partner.

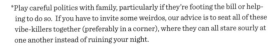

*Play careful politics with family, particularly if they're footing the bill or help-ing to do so. If you have to invite some weirdos, our advice is to seat all of these vibe-killers together (preferably in a corner), where they can all stare sourly at one another instead of ruining your night.

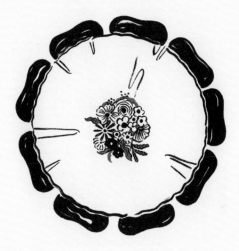

A Recipe for a Perfect Seating Chart

The seating chart is a complicated yet crucial part of wedding planning. Just as your guest list should represent a perfect mix of friends, family, party people, and chill people, your seating chart should scramble all of those guests into the proper permutations to yield maximum fun.

01. Give each individual on your guest list a "personality score" between 1 and 5 (5 being life of the party, 1 being—for lack of a better term—kinda boring).

02. Distribute personalities as evenly as possible among tables. Try to put at least one high-scoring guest at every table; their dazzling personalities will rub off on the less personable people around them. (Contrary to popular belief, personality is just as infectious as strep or the flu—simply being exposed to it will do the trick for most people.)

03. Are you just assigning your guests to tables, or to specific seats at the table? If seats are assigned, try to put single guests together for maximum matchmaking opportunities. Everyone loves a good wedding hookup story.

04. If you manage to have any guests who actually score less than 1 on the personality scale (hey, we all have a bigoted uncle who clocks in at about a 0.3), we feel for you. Just seat them next to each other! Misery loves company.

GET YOUR CATERER TO SPILL THE BEANS—AND OTHER TIPS

ALL VENDORS ARE not created equal. Find the right ones for your wedding by asking the right questions.

DJ

There's more to being a wedding DJ than making a playlist of great music—it takes experience and finesse. Ask your DJ candidates how many weddings they've done. Confirm that they take requests, and that you won't need to pay extra if your favorite songs aren't already in their music library.

Live Band

If you're considering a particular band, watch videos of their work online or—better yet—try to catch them live. Ask if they act as emcee, introducing events (first dance, cake cutting, etc.) and making announcements throughout the night. If there are songs you'd like to hear and they don't play them, find out if they would be willing to learn them. Also check on how often they take breaks.

Photographer

Experienced wedding photographers will have portfolios of their work, and what you see is what you'll get. Find a photographer that shoots the style you want (portraiture, documentary, or fine art, to name a few) then find out exactly what is offered and included in packages, and whether they follow a shot list. It's also worth asking whether retouching and color correcting are included.

"After a good dinner one can forgive anybody, even one's own relatives."

—OSCAR WILDE

Caterer

Schedule a tasting with a potential caterer before you hire, and ask them what they specialize in before you discuss the options you're most interested in. You'll likely have guests with food allergies or dietary restrictions, so find out how they accommodate those needs. Ask whether they prepare food on site—if so, you'll need to confirm your venue has the necessary facilities. If presentation is important to you, request photos. And definitely get the scoop on whether they provide dinnerware, bartenders or servers.

Baker

Like the caterer, always arrange a cake tasting with your prospective baker before you hire one. Ask to see examples of their work that fall within your budget (guest count may affect this). Find out if they can recreate your dream cake from a photo, or customize your cake to match your wedding colors or theme. Be sure to confirm whether the top tier of the cake is included in pricing (it costs extra). If you'd like a groom's cake, ask if they offer any packages.

Florist

Find out if the florist will set up and remove arrangements, or if they only drop off the flowers. Ask them what happens to the display materials, vases, and stands after the wedding. These arrangements often disappear with guests, and if they need to go back, your wedding planner will need to keep an eye out. Speaking of wedding planners...

Wedding Planner

This is the one vendor to rule them all, so it's especially important that they share your vision for style and budget. If you're not sure where to start with some of your other vendors, ask your potential wedding planner if they have a recommended list and if they can get you discounts. Ask if they'll attend meetings with your other vendors. Discuss the guest list and how RSVPs will be managed. If you're planning a destination wedding, ask them for examples of destination weddings they have planned.

In addition to the pre-wedding phase, find out whether your planner will handle day-of coordination. Will they build a timeline that explains what everyone needs to do, and when, on the wedding day? Their experience is crucial in realistically estimating how long everything will take (and allowing extra time for emergencies).

Questions to Ask Every Vendor

→ How many weddings have you done?

→ Are you available on my wedding date?

→ Have you worked at my venue before?

→ How do deposits and payments work?

→ Do you have other weddings booked on the same day as mine?

→ What happens if you are sick or unable to work on my wedding day?

BREAK BREAD (AND THE ICE)

REHEARSAL DINNERS technically exist to run through the ceremony the night before the actual ceremony—to make sure everyone knows what they should do, where they should be, and generally how not to eff up your wedding. But let's be real: Unless your ceremony is going to be super complicated—with multiple readers, rituals, and children involved—most adults can handle walking in a straight line without a tutorial.

THE REAL REASONS REHEARSAL DINNERS EXIST:

01. As a thank you to the wedding party for being in your ceremony (the rehearsal dinner is also a great time to hand out the wedding party gifts—yes, you need to get each of your groomsmen a small "thank you" gift).

02. For your family and your partner's family to better get to know each other before the big day (a.k.a. "The part where you and your partner's moms get white-wine drunk together").

03. To share a delicious meal. Restaurant, buffet, backyard BBQ, beach bonfire with a few extra large pizzas, takeout burgers—your rehearsal dinner doesn't have to be fancy; it just has to be a bonding experience (but if you have to reserve a venue, do so four to six months in advance).

04. To lighten the load of necessary talks/toasts at your actual wedding reception. If you're worried you won't be able to control who grabs the mic at your reception, it might be smart to have "open mic toasting" at the rehearsal dinner instead (let 'em get it out of their system the night before).

05. To have fun, let off steam, and spend some quality time with the people closest to you before the actual wedding. Amid the day-of commotion (and having to make the "thank you" rounds at the reception like a pageant queen), you probably won't get to spend much time with any one particular guest or family member. Now's your chance.

Groom Service

YOU'RE ALL ON THE LIST

If possible, extend your rehearsal dinner invitations beyond your families, wedding party, and out-of-towners, and include your entire guest list in the festivities. Bringing all of your guests together the night before the wedding will get the ice breaking out of the way early—which means that by the time your reception rolls around, they'll already be BFFs and go straight to the dance floor to embarrass themselves, instead of wasting an hour on introductions. If hosting an extra dinner for your entire guest list isn't something you can or want to do, then just casually invite everyone to meet you at a bar after the rehearsal, and drink away the social awkwardness before your big day.

REMEMBER

Family doesn't have to be "twice removed" to be removed from your guest list.

Stand your ground and surround yourself with the people who are most important to you.

3

During the Wedding

All that blood, sweat, and vendor booking you put into planning your wedding is the difficult part—enjoying it shouldn't be too hard for you. However, there will still be a lot going on that day—groomsmen to wrangle, people to thank, photos to pose for, details to pay attention to, and duh, beautiful memories to be made. Here's how to find some day-of-zen.

"The universe doesn't allow perfection."

–STEPHEN HAWKING

SHOULD YOU HIRE A DAY-OF WEDDING COORDINATOR?

SHORT ANSWER: YES. If you decide to forgo the wedding planner, or if the planner you've chosen doesn't offer day-of coordination services, hire someone to manage the details of your big day. A day-of wedding coordinator handles the little things (making sure the table settings are right), the big things (what to do if the bride gets a stain on her dress five minutes before the ceremony), and the awkward things (approaching party crashers who are ordering drinks at the bar and asking them to leave).

Your wedding is your special day—but you're also the host. You won't be able to have fun at your own party if you're obsessing over the details, so just pay a professional to do it.

What to Make Sure You Do on Your Wedding Day

CHECKLIST	✓
Eat breakfast	☐
Kill the rehearsal-dinner hangover (if you paced yourself and don't have one, congratulations—we're not all as smart as you are)	☐
Review your schedule for the day	☐
Make sure you're packed for your honeymoon	☐
Write out a list of people you need to talk to/thank/dance with at the reception	☐
Double check with the best man that he has the rings	☐
Triple check that everyone knows where they need to be and when	☐
Relax with a favorite cocktail—but don't get drunk before the ceremony	☐
Corral the groomsmen—make sure to ask them to meet you where you're staying early	☐
Have a moment of zen	☐
Reread and reflect upon your wedding vows	☐
Give yourself plenty of time to get ready	☐
Write a thoughtful note to your partner and have a groomsman deliver it	☐
Make a thank-you toast at the reception	☐
Arrange with caterers to take your dinner to-go (many couples don't get more than a few bites in at the reception)	☐
Coordinate group photos at the reception—there are plenty of friends you'll want a pic with who won't be included in the cocktail hour photos with the families and wedding party	☐
Have a moment with each of your parents at the reception	☐
Run away with your new bride for a half-hour	☐
Dance your ass off	☐
Drink a lot of water	☐
Eat something before you drunkenly collapse at the end of the night—you don't want to spend your first day as a married man throwing up or with a throbbing headache	☐

YOUR SUIT PANTS DON'T HAVE CARGO POCKETS

WHAT SHOULD YOU CARRY in your pockets on your wedding day? As little as possible, and definitely not your phone. You also don't want any lumpy pants or bulky pockets showing up in the wedding photos. Our advice is to keep it simple: Take your vows, notes for your toast, and a list of people you need to thank and leave the rest at the hotel; your friends will have you covered.

Groom Service

PUT YOUR PHONE DOWN

You hired a professional photographer. Your guests brought their phones and are taking tons of pictures. They're posting these pictures to Instagram and Facebook and are using your personalized wedding hashtag. Seriously: Don't bring your phone to your wedding. Live in your moment, and let everyone else document it. Posting pictures to social media is something you do when you're wasting time at work, not when you're celebrating one of the best days of your life.

Wedding Disasters and How to Deal with Them

No matter how much you plan, shit can and will go wrong on your wedding day. Some things you can't control (the weather, other people)—it's better just to accept it. Know this: No matter what happens, your life will go on, and you and your partner will still be married and in love at the end of the day. Even if it rains, even if the best man gets drunk and makes an embarrassing speech, even if the fire department gets called (let's hope not). All you can do is laugh it off and focus on the good parts. At least you'll get a story out of it, like these people did...

SOME LIKE IT HOT

"Wedding in Mexico, in July. It was actually so hot that after the ceremony everyone had sweat through all of their clothes—kind of awkward and embarrassing, especially for people with light colors on."

Lesson learned: Cover your entire body in antiperspirant or find a shady spot.

NON-FUNCTIONAL ART

"A close friend of mine drank too much at a wedding once, and went over to a bench to lay down. The bench broke. It turned out it wasn't an ordinary bench—it was an expensive work of art. The bride's father got upset once he heard how much this would cost."

Lesson learned: Keep the priceless artwork far, far away from the open bar.

HOW LOW CAN YOU GO?

"The groom got a little too low on the dance floor and pulled a muscle in his leg. He had to be wheelchaired to the wedding suite by the bride. They were both still in good spirits!"

Lesson learned: This guy is our wedding hero. Be like this guy.

NO SHOES, NO CEREMONY

"The bride was going for the 'boho' vibe and was at the wedding barefoot. Someone (who I assume had a bit too much tequila) dropped their beer bottle on the dance floor and proceeded to kick the bottle and the shards around so that no one would notice. About 10 minutes later, the bride stepped on a massive piece of glass while dancing and it lodged into her foot. Needless to say, there was panic and a lot of gauze was needed."

Lesson learned: Probably keep your shoes on?

FEELING FAINT

"I was at a wedding where a bridesmaid fainted during the ceremony. It was literally 'we now pronounce you husband and wife'...thud. She had poor circulation in her legs, and was wearing her heels for a bit longer than anticipated. They wound up having to take her away in an ambulance. Poor girl missed all of the formal pictures and most of the reception."

Lesson learned: Nothing, we just feel sorry for her...

"WITH THIS RING, I THEE... WHAT?"

"My husband was the best man at a wedding. A few days before, the groom was at the gym lifting weights and, crushed his hand in between two weights. The main casualty was the ring finger of his left hand. The groom had to wrap it in a splint for the ceremony, and the bride had to put the ring on his right hand instead."

Lesson learned: Cool it on the strenuous exercise during the week before the wedding.

KNOW YOUR LIMITS

"Wedding in Cabo. Worst best man speech you could ever imagine. Took over the mic and used it as his therapy outlet. Discussed how this was his only vacation that year, and was completely intoxicated the entire time. How did it end? He got kicked out of the wedding by the father of the bride."

Lesson learned: Keep your friends close and your best man sober (at least until after he gives his toast).

(4)

After the Wedding

You did it. You're married.

You made a public commitment to the person of
your dreams, and partied late into the
night with your best friends and family. Even
better, the best (read: the honeymoon) is
yet to come—but you'll have to make it through
that brunch hangover first.

AN ODE TO BRUNCH

Hour of pain,
Hangover of sorrow and death.
What angel lies hidden behind the sunglass?
What perfect spread will whisper the mem'ry of celebration shared?
Who shall banish the thought of stained dress shirt?

Not for a single moment, Brunch, lovely meal,
have I ceased to see my flute topped with champagne,
nor lonely celery stalk overtaken with bloody mix.
Not for a single moment, gathering of friends,
who in mountains of bacon, fruit, and scramble,
abandon dozing in bed with toothbrush unpasted.

And you, lovely Brunch, rejuvenate the soul,
with your table and hands open.
Bland pancake and waffle denied their seat,
for salty, savory, sweet comrades to guard against the doldrums,
and giddy puppy's hair to renew festivity,
inspire the spirit, and erase agony.

YOU SHOULD TAKE THAT HONEYMOON NOW

YOUR WEDDING WON'T feel like real life. It will feel like some weird, alternate universe version of your life where everything looks perfect, the drinks are constantly flowing and your creepy uncle is dancing with your partner's younger sister, but for some reason it's socially acceptable. So why not keep living that weird, alternate-universe life for as long as possible? Pushing your honeymoon back means returning to office emails and cleaning your apartment—it means shattering the wedding fantasy. Leaving for your honeymoon right after the big day prolongs that weird, amazing wedding universe for a little bit longer—only it's way better because your family isn't there.

Your Honeymoon Out of Office Playbook

X

To: <All Office>
Subject: Automatic Reply: "Out of Office ✈"

Thanks for your email. I'm currently out of office on my honeymoon, and will contact you if I ever return, which is a 50% chance at best.

Thanks,
[Your Name Here]

X

To: <All Office>
Subject: Automatic Reply: "OOO"

I'm OOO on my honeymoon right now. Unfortunately, I'll be back on 5/27. Contact me then.

Thank You,
[Your Name Here]

X

To: <All Office>
Subject: Automatic Reply: "OOO: Poolside"

Thanks for your message. I'm really busy sipping a margarita by a pool right now, so I won't have time to get to it for awhile.

♥,
[Your Name Here]

X

To: <All Office>
Subject: Automatic Reply: "Out of Office"

I'm currently OOO on my honeymoon until June 24th, with limited access to email. If it's an emergency, why are you contacting me in the first place? Call 911.

Godspeed,
[Your Name Here]

X

To: <All Office>
Subject: Automatic Reply: "OOO"

I'm out of office on my honeymoon until July 12th. It's beautiful here. So how's your cubicle?

X

To: <All Office>
Subject: Automatic Reply: "❀❀❀OOO❀❀❀"

I'm currently OOO on my honeymoon. I have access to internet but will only be using it to post vacation pics. Contact me after the 22nd.

Sincerely,
[Your Name Here]

What to Do with That Terabyte of Wedding Photos

You're going to get a whole mess of photos back from your photographers. They'll look great, you'll look great, your partner will look great—but what do you do with all of them?

FRAME THEM

Put a few photos in frames and display them on a bedside table or in a hallway. But don't go overboard—20 framed photos hanging in your living room will make it look like a wedding shrine.

SEND COPIES TO FAMILY

Real talk: Most people probably won't care about receiving copies of your wedding photos, but your family kind of has to (and your mom actually will). Send relatives physical copies of the wedding photos focused on their side of the family. Frame them if you want to go the extra mile.

MAKE AN ALBUM

Maybe a photo album is included with the photography package you ordered. If not, you and your partner can make your own. An album is a nice keepsake that you'll probably look at a lot during the first few months after your wedding—and then put on a shelf and completely forget about in the years to come.

POST THEM TO SOCIAL MEDIA

Take your favorite photos—including some that were shot by your friends—and post them to social media. Also make a more extensive Facebook album for your aunts in Idaho who'll actually take the time to click through 100 photos and leave embarrassing comments on each one.

Consider What You Will (and Should) Save

There are plenty of artifacts you can save from your wedding—invitations, menus, pressed flowers from the bouquet. Include them in that wedding album that you're never going to look at. (Hey, maybe your kids will want to flip through it 20 years from now?)

On the other end of the spectrum, you may opt not to save any keepsakes from your wedding. That's okay, too. Let the day live on in your memories, not in physical totems. How Buddhist of you.

PIECE OF CAKE
TIME TO SAY "THANK YOU"

Thank you notes should be sent out within three months after the ceremony, to everyone who touched your wedding in some way: the wedding party, the guests, even the vendors. They should be hand written and personalized. If you miss the three-month mark, remember: Better late than never. Sending thank-you notes a year after the wedding is a dick move, but less so than no thank-you note at all.

ANNIVERSARY GIFTS BY YEAR

CELEBRATING EACH YEAR OF MARRIAGE WITH THE GIFT of a particular material dates back to the Victorian era. Increasingly durable gifts given each year represent the progressive strengthening of the marriage. Cool symbolism, but why not try these modern alternatives instead (or make up your own)?

ANNIVERSARY	TRADITIONAL GIFT	ALTERNATIVE GIFT
FIRST YEAR	Paper	A handwritten letter
SECOND YEAR	Cotton	A favorite meal
THIRD YEAR	Leather	Really nice booze
FOURTH YEAR	Fruit	Dream concert tickets
FIFTH YEAR	Wood	A trip to an exotic locale
10TH YEAR	Tin	You can never take enough trips to exotic locales...
25TH YEAR	Silver	Matching midlife-crisis cars (may we suggest red convertibles?)
50TH YEAR	Gold	A really nice walker and/or cane (bonus points if you combine both the traditional and alternative options and go for a gold-plated walker and/or cane)

Anniversary Traditions

TRY:
MESSAGE IN A BOTTLE

At your reception, ask guests to write notes on little pieces of paper and put them into a glass bottle that you and your partner will open on your first anniversary. You'll undoubtedly be moved to tears, laughs, and maybe even a few raised eyebrows when you read your guests' messages a year later.

DO NOT TRY:
EAT YEAR-OLD WEDDING CAKE

Many couples freeze the top tier of their wedding cake to eat on their first anniversary. Let's face it: This is pretty gross. Just go out to dinner and order a less-ancient dessert on your anniversary instead. (Or have your cake maker bake an anniversary cake; some even include this as part of the package.)

TRY: RECREATE YOUR
WEDDING MEAL

Bring back the food and (hazy, drunken) memories of your reception. Recreate your First Supper (your wedding meal) every year on your anniversary—either by preparing the same foods at home, or going to the restaurant that catered your wedding.

Ceremony

Making it official without officially going insane.

1

Here Comes the Guide

It's easy to get caught up in planning the reception, but don't forget why you, your partner, and your guests are getting together, dressing up, and spending money in the first place. Attendees will remember a good ceremony for years, while you and your spouse will remember it for a lifetime. Standing before your family and friends to publicly declare your love and commitment to each other is a beautiful experience—but there are also a hell of a lot of decisions to make before that moment. In the following pages, we'll help you and your partner narrow down your options.

"Must go faster."

—JEFF GOLDBLUM
AS DR. IAN MALCOLM IN
JURASSIC PARK

CEREMONIES: WHAT TO EXPECT

WE PROBABLY DON'T NEED TO EXPLAIN MUCH HERE, because chances are you've been in a wedding—or at least attended one—before. But for the small percentage of adult humans who have never been involved in celebrating the union of two individuals in holy matrimony, there's a general formula these events tend to follow. Depending on religion, culture, or personal preference, your mileage may vary.

PROCESSIONAL

A fancy word for when the wedding party walks down the aisle.

OFFICIANT'S OPENING REMARKS

"Dearly beloved, we are gathered here today..." and all that stuff you've seen in the movies.

Groom Service

WEDDING SECURITY

A smart seating chart should reduce family fights at the reception. If the gloves come off earlier, pre-approve your best man to take a few groomsmen and sort 'em out. Because what are groomsmen if not really well-dressed bouncers?

THE COUPLE'S STORY

The officiant's heart-tingling speech about how the couple met, their values, and hopes for the future. If people are alternating between laughing, tearing up, and laughing-while-tearing-up, the officiant is knocking it out of the park.

READINGS

Inspiring passages chosen by the couple or officiant, read by the officiant or a designated "reader." They can be religious, spiritual, poetic, or even a quote from a favorite movie or book.

Continued on the next page

MEANINGFUL SYMBOLIC ACTS

Ring a bell. Light a candle. Mix sand. Release some poor, confused doves into the wild. These are but a few of the meaningful, symbolic acts that some couples choose to include in their weddings. Of course, many religions and cultures have their own rituals—or make up your own.

THE EXCHANGE OF VOWS

Maybe the couple goes the traditional "to have and to hold" route, or maybe they've written their own vows. Either way, they'll exchange them now.

EXCHANGE OF RINGS

"With this ring, I thee wed," and more stuff you've definitely seen in the movies. Basically a call-and-response, repeat-after-me thing between you, your partner, and the officiant. Focus.

THE KISS

A.K.A. "the moment everyone's been waiting for." We certainly hope that you don't need an explanation for this one, but here goes: little or no tongue is preferred, but for the love of matrimony, let's have some lip-to-lip contact. You can dip, you can smile—have some fun with it.

CLOSING REMARKS

The officiant pronounces the couple as married, makes a few closing remarks (or, in a religious ceremony, a blessing), and then releases everyone so the party can start.

RECESSIONAL

A fancy word for when the wedding party, followed by the newlyweds, depart from the ceremony.

REMEMBER

Pinterest is not a wedding planner.

Do It Yourself, just don't do it by yourself.

THE TRUTH BEHIND TRADITION

WE'RE ALL FAMILIAR WITH THE TYPICAL ceremony traditions—especially those related to the bride: the white dress and veil, the bouquet, and "something borrowed." As you plan your wedding, use this guide to decide if these traditions, even stripped of their original intent, belong in your ceremony.

WHY THE BRIDE'S FATHER WALKS HER DOWN THE AISLE

Back when arranged marriages were de rigueur, daughters were considered their fathers' property. Dad would trade his daughter's hand for money, land, or social status to a man he deemed acceptable.

WHY SHE WEARS A VEIL AND A WHITE DRESS

Queen Victoria started the tradition of wearing a white dress, symbolizing purity and chastity. The veil originated to identify brides as a virgin (or not). Our thoughts? It's a little unfair that the groom doesn't have to wear a wardrobe declaring his virginity (or not). Overall, that's too much information for your average guest.

SOMETHING OLD, SOMETHING NEW, SOMETHING BORROWED, SOMETHING BLUE

This is a Victorian era custom that stuck, and each item (old, new, borrowed, blue) supposedly symbolizes optimism, love, purity and basically good vibes. It's a fun tradition if you don't bank on the superstition of it. Traditionally this applied only to the bride, but it could be modified for groom using items from their brothers, fathers, or grandfathers.

WHY THE BRIDE CARRIES A BOUQUET

This is tied to the reason June is such a popular month for weddings. In the 15th and 16th centuries, folks would only take baths annually—yes, once per year—in the month of May. So at these June weddings, people wouldn't smell as much like death. To aid in masking B.O., the bride would pick a fresh bouquet of flowers on the way to the ceremony.

ORIGINS OF "TYING THE KNOT" AND "GETTING HITCHED"

This comes from one of two traditions. Ancient Romans would tie the bride's girdle in knots, forcing the groom to untie those knots before consummating the marriage. Another possibility: the Celtic tradition of handfasting, which entails binding the hands of the bride and groom together during the ceremony, only to be untied once the marriage was consummated. (Are you starting to notice how much other people wanted the bride and groom to have sex?)

"Yesterday's weirdness is tomorrow's reason why."

–HUNTER S. THOMPSON

ORIGINS OF THE BRIDAL SHOWER

Again, *when daughters were considered property,* fathers would sweeten the deal for the groom by including a dowry of money, land, or livestock. If the father didn't approve of the groom, he might withhold the dowry. Bridal showers were created in the 16th century as an alternative, with friends and family giving small gifts as a replacement for the dowry so the couple could still wed. Hooray for crowdsourcing!

WHY DIAMOND ENGAGEMENT RINGS

In 1477, one of the first recorded diamond engagement rings came from a nervous Archduke named Max (okay, Maximilian). Most folks currently blame De Beers, which controlled an estimated 90 percent of the world's diamond production by 1890—the rest is marketing. In any case, don't hate the player—hate the game. Or better yet, discuss ring-related expectations before you pop the question.

WHY WE WEAR WEDDING RINGS

Couples in ancient Egyptian and Roman cultures were the earliest to exchange and wear rings as a symbol of eternity, as the circle never ends. Unless you lose it.

WHY WEDDING RINGS ARE WORN ON THE LEFT-HAND RING FINGER

Two Latin words: *vena amoris* (vein of love). Back when the jury was still out on whether the world was flat, it was believed that the vein of the fourth (ring) finger ran directly to the heart. Turns out all fingers have the same vein structure, but the engagement and wedding rings still sit on lefty #4.

PIECE OF CAKE
HOW TO DEAL WITH NERVES

Your wedding day will be full of uncertainties, but one thing you can be sure about is that you will feel like you're going to throw up or have a heart attack—maybe both at the same time. No, it's not a rehearsal dinner hangover. It's nerves, and they happen to everyone who is about to publicly make a really important life transition. Take a deep breath, have a moment of zen before the ceremony—maybe this means meditation, or giving yourself a pep talk in the mirror (do people actually do that?), or having exactly one cocktail (we all have our "things")—and laser-focus on your partner throughout the day. That's your ally, and you two are in this together.

AN ODE TO
THE RING BEARER

O little Ring Bearer, mem'ry of youth,
Harken to days, when my tree of life in full foliage,
Coin and care earn'd only by my after-school snack

Thou, wearing tiny tuxedo, wand'ring to and fro,
Picking thy nose whilst photo flash blinds,
A moment for eternity; a booger for the ages

The impulse of thy youth, our missing rings,
My wife, O Uncontrollable! If even gem is found
In boyhood haunts, and can be salvaged

Wild Spirit, which art moving everywhere;
Destroyer and weeper; hear, O Hear! Stop thy tears,
Rings concealed in diaper soiled. All is forgiven.

The Official Officiant's Guide

How important is the officiant's role in your ceremony? Let's put it this way: They set the tone for the entire wedding. Consult these pages when making the very important decision of who should play master of ceremonies at your wedding—then give that person our handy tear-out instructional to make sure they don't screw it up.

HOW TO CHOOSE AN OFFICIANT

A GREAT OFFICIANT WILL HAVE ENOUGH CHARISMA to keep guests' minds from wandering to dark places like, "When does the reception start?" But there's more to an officiant than public speaking skills. Here's all you need to consider when choosing one.

Things to Consider

DECIDE WHAT KIND OF OFFICIANT YOU WOULD LIKE TO WORK WITH

Minister, priest, rabbi, justice of the peace, family member, friend, or any combination of the aforementioned—the possibilities are almost endless, stopping only at "your dog."

PRO TIP: If you're planning on deviating from the traditional wedding, you can't assume that a religious officiant will adapt their ceremony to your wishes. Understand their parameters before you hire them.

CHOOSE SOMEONE YOU CONNECT WITH

Weddings are stressful enough as it is. The last thing you need is to be married by someone who makes you feel awkward.

PRO TIP: If you opt for an officiant outside of your personal contacts, start looking at least nine months in advance so you have time to get to know them. Meet candidates in person, and make sure you have natural chemistry.

**FIND OUT HOW MUCH INPUT
YOU CAN HAVE IN THE
CEREMONY**

It's your wedding, so you should
have control over the rituals,
readings, and ceremony, right? This
isn't the case with some traditional
religious services. Find an officiant (religious or otherwise) who
will adapt to your needs.

PRO TIP: If there's anything that
irks you about traditional weddings
(e.g., the phrase "till death do us
part" being grim… because it kind
of is), be vocal about it. Make a
"no-go" list for your officiant that
includes language or topics you're
not willing to budge on.

MAKE SURE IT'S LEGAL

Every state has different qualifica-
tions for officiants. For many, it's
as simple as becoming an ordained
minister through the Universal Life
Church. Your chosen officiant can
do it online, for free, while eating
BBQ chips and wearing their pajamas.
It's that easy.

PRO TIP: In addition to making sure
your officiant is legally qualified,
call your county clerk to check if
they require any additional paper-
work besides your marriage license.

GET IT IN WRITING

This doesn't necessarily need to be
in the form of a contract (especially if your officiant is a friend
or family member), but at least an
email detailing exactly where, when,
and what can be a life-saver amidst
the stress of wedding planning.

PRO TIP: Shit happens. Be sure to
work out a back-up plan with your
officiant, in the very rare event
that they need to cancel last
minute.

Ceremonies are like Pauly Shore movies: the shorter the better.

Choose your readings accordingly.

HOW TO BECOME A KICKASS OFFICIANT

CONGRATULATIONS! You've been asked to officiate a wedding for the first time ever. The couple selected you because you're special to them, but—perhaps more importantly—they asked you because they believe you have enough pizzazz to make their wedding a touching, memorable, totally un-boring experience. Uh, that's a lot of pressure. But you can do it. Just trust us and follow these guidelines.

Get ordained

The first step in officiating a ceremony is becoming official. In many states, it's as simple as registering online with the Universal Life Church (it's free, and like the easiest thing you'll ever do). Other states may allow you to get a special one-day permit. Go online and research the laws in the state where the wedding is taking place to see what's required of you.

Talk to the couple about what they want

You're a friend or family member of the couple, so you probably already have an idea of what they would like (or freak out over). But people (understandably) get very particular about their weddings, so take time to sit down with them and ask about these key components of the ceremony:

SPECTRUM OF TRADITIONALNESS

Stick to the tried-and-true "dearly beloved" script, toss it, or do a combo of traditional and modern? Ask them in detail about what they like and don't like.

On a scale of 1 to 10, how traditional does the couple want their ceremony to be?

1 —— 2 —— 3 —— 4 —— 5 —— 6 —— 7 —— 8 —— 9 —— 10

Notes: _____

_____

_____

Continued on the next page

Talk to the couple about what they want (cont.)

TONE

What are the couple's thoughts on tone?

a.) Romantic

b.) Serious

c.) Funny

d.) Seriously funny

e.) Combo of the above

f.) Other: _____

Notes: _____

_____

_____

LENGTH

How long does the couple want your speech to be? (In our experience, a balance between "short and sweet" and "substantial enough to have meaning" is usually best.)

Couple's ideal speech length: _____ minutes

Notes: _____

_____

_____

THE COUPLE'S STORY

Some couples meet under less than fairy-tale circumstances. If the couple met at a frat party while they were both wearing slutty jungle animal costumes, would they be fine with you sharing this story with wedding guests, or would they be embarrassed by it? Set some boundaries here.

Notes: _____

_____

_____

READINGS

Is the couple choosing the wedding readings, or are they leaving it in your hands? Do they have any pieces of writing, songs, or quotes that are important to them?

Notes: _____

_____

_____

Write your ceremony script

Now that you know more about what the couple wants from you, it's time to sit down and write this mofo (excuse us, we meant to say, "the most beautiful wedding ceremony of all time"). Start with a basic wedding ceremony script (you can find one online), just to get a reference for the pacing and basic steps in a ceremony. Edit and add to it based on the previous conversations you've had with the couple about what they want.

QUESTIONS TO ASK YOURSELF

What is your relationship to them and why is it important?

How do you know the couple?

How have you seen their relationship evolve over time?

What is your favorite story or experience you've had with the couple?

What are your wishes for the couples future together?

Why are they perfect for each other?

Continued on the next page

Ceremony script outline

In general, your ceremony script should probably follow this order (again, unless the couple has stated otherwise):

MAKE A FEW OPENING REMARKS

Welcome and thank everyone for sharing in the couple's special day (in a traditional ceremony, this would be the "Dearly beloved" part).

SAY SOME GENERAL WORDS ABOUT LOVE AND COMMITMENT

Remind everyone that's why you're here today.

TELL THE COUPLE'S LOVE STORY

Here's where you have the most room to play. Make it personal and add elements of your relationship to the couple (remember, they asked you to be their officiant for a reason). Consider the questions on the page when writing this part.

PRESENT THE WEDDING READINGS

Could be read by you, the couple, or another special person chosen by the couple. As we mentioned earlier, discuss the couple's ideas for this part of the ceremony ahead of time.

VOWS. RINGS. KISS.

You'll either conduct the traditional vows, or maybe the couple has written their own.

SAY YOUR THANK-YOUS AND CLOSING REMARKS

Pronounce the couple as married, thank everyone again for sharing in this special moment, and release them all to the reception.

That's it! You're done writing The Best Ceremony Script in All of Wedding History (or at least pretty close to it).

Stuff you probably shouldn't forget to do

Now that you've actually written the ceremony, give some consideration to these other factors before the big day arrives.

CROSS-REFERENCE YOUR REMARKS WITH THE COUPLE'S VOWS

If the couple are writing their own vows, meet with them beforehand to make sure their vows don't clash with (or aren't repetitive of) what you're planning on saying. Hearing the same thing three times over is a recipe for awkwardness and boredom.

BRUSH UP ON YOUR PUBLIC SPEAKING SKILLS

Unfortunately, a flawlessly written, heartstring-pulling speech is only half the officiant battle. You also need to know how to work a crowd but not be so much of a scene-stealer that you outshine the couple. It's a fine line.

DON'T FORGET TO:

→ Practice reading your speech aloud in the days before the wedding
→ Make eye contact

→ Smile
→ Stand up straight
→ Don't speak too fast
→ Don't speak in monotone

These are all totally "duh" things, but they can be easy to forget in the moment. Practice over and over until you've got this thing nailed, and maybe meditate and/or have a drink before you take to the altar.

FIGURE OUT WHAT TO WEAR TO THIS THING

Ask the couple whether they'd like you to wear anything in particular—they'll probably have a dress code they want you to follow, or at least a few opinions about it. On the rare occasion that they don't, we wouldn't advise wearing anything too "statement." You obviously want to look top of your game because you're going to be in a lot of the wedding photos, but you definitely don't want to distract from the couple on their special day.

SLAY IT

The day has arrived. You're an ordained minister. You look good, feel good, and are ready to wow this audience and give the couple the amazing wedding memories they deserve. The altar awaits your sparkling stage presence. Let's do this.

③ # Make it Super

If you think of your ceremony as a burrito, some things—like the ring exchange—would be considered "rice and beans": tried-and-true staples in every wedding. The items detailed in the following pages could be better classified as "add-ons"—the guacamole, sour cream, and pico de gallo that will take your wedding from regular to super. And as with a burrito, there's no one right way to build your ceremony. It's about creating the perfect combo of flavors to best please your taste buds (or, you know, yours, your partner's, and your guests'). So, from readings to processional music, we present to you a buffet of optional wedding ingredients: choose to your liking, roll them up in the tortilla that is your ceremony, and enjoy.

WRITING YOUR OWN VOWS

IF YOU AND YOUR BETROTHED HAVE agreed to write vows, you'll need to put your promises on paper. There is technically no wrong way to do this, but we've developed an approach that should set you up for success. *Step by Step* was a "modestly amusing" television series starring Patrick Duffy and Suzanne Somers (*Variety*, 1991), and it's also a great way to approach writing your vows. Follow the outline below for a fail-proof, bona fide tear-jerker that will leave both your partner and your guests happy-crying on the big day. Let's get started.

Basic Vow Anatomy

BEGINNING	Past: How did you meet? When did you know it was serious? What challenges have you faced together?
MIDDLE	Present: What brought you to this day? How do you feel about marrying your partner? What's the one thing you want to tell them on your wedding day?
END	Future: Goals you want to achieve with your partner and the future you see together. Probably mention love here. And insert 3 to 4 promises here.
CURTAIN CALL	Everyone cries. Maintain eye contact, but not obsessively (that would be creepy).

Continued on the next page

Let's Write Your Vows

Now that you know the basic structure for your vows, it's time to get into the details. Follow these pro tips (especially the part about this not being the time or place to finally debut the stand-up comedy routine you've been practicing in your head for three years—trust us on this one), and show everyone exactly why you are marriage material.

STUDY UP

Read some traditional vows—these could be of any religion or culture. You can also YouTube vows written by couples to get a feel for the length and structure. Think about the kinds of promises these couples are making to one another.

REFLECT ON YOUR RELATIONSHIP

Get sentimental. Gather 5 to 10 of your favorite memories from your time together: what drew you to your partner, the ways you've supported each other, and why you think you'll make a great husband.

TONE IS IMPORTANT

It's great to throw in a quick, good-natured joke, but this isn't the time to channel your inner Seinfeld ("What's the deal with the little flowers on my jacket?"). Ideally, your vows will be equal parts touching, funny, and hopeful for your future.

MAKE SOME PROMISES

Finesse those memories and ideas into promises. Three or four should do it.

OUTLINE IT

Make an outline. Feel free to map out your vows as you see fit. Our example (see page 69) works well, every time.

EDIT WHAT YOU JUST WROTE

Remove 90 percent of the inside jokes you find, and remove anything that would embarrass you, your family, and, most importantly, your partner.

QUALITY, NOT QUANTITY!

Err on the side of brevity. So edit, edit, and edit some more.

MAKE A CLEAN COPY

Does it look good? Great! Print out a shiny new, legible copy and keep the draft on your computer for further edits and more copies.

PRACTICE MAKES PERFECT

Find a mirror and read your vows aloud. If something is clunky or off, you'll hear it as you read. Make notes as you go for minor adjustments. Then do it again with the changes.

MAKE YOUR FINAL COPY, AND PAT YOURSELF ON THE BACK

Even if you decide to memorize them, keep a copy of your vows on you during the ceremony just in case.

EXTRA CREDIT

On your wedding day, remember that you're just talking to your fiancé. Don't let the (possibly hundreds of) other humans steal your focus—you wrote this for your partner.

READ IT AND WEEP (TEARS OF JOY)

YOU WON'T FIND READINGS IN EVERY WEDDING, but when they're done right, they add an unrivaled layer of emotional depth to the ceremony.

Many couples opt for religious or spiritual readings, but if those aren't your thing, try a poem, song lyrics, a passage from a favorite novel, a quote from the movie you saw on your first date (hopefully it wasn't part of the *Transformers* series), or even some lines from that TV show you're always binge watching together (okay, this one seems pretty weird, but we don't want to rule it out altogether).

The ideal wedding reading is…

TIMELESS

Yeah, it sounds cool within the context of the page, or the song, or the movie, but can people understand your passage when you separate it from the original source and plop it in your wedding?

SHORT

Ideal length is around 2 minutes. Anything shorter may not feel impactful enough, while a longer reading might result in guests spacing out, thus killing your magic moment.

RELEVANT

Your reading doesn't have to be gag-inducingly cute, flowery, or romantic (unless you want it to be!), but it should probably at least have something to do with marriage, love, or partnership. It is a wedding, after all!

PERSONAL

Above all, your reading should mean something to you and your partner. Make it yours, even if that does mean reciting a monologue from your favorite TV show.

Groom Service

HIGH-STAKES WEDDING IMPROV

Some couples also let their officiant (or another special person) select and perform the readings for their wedding—and surprise the couple with their selections at the altar (gulp). Not knowing in advance what's going to be read in your ceremony may be high risk, but it's also high reward. Nothing beats being surprised with thoughtful, heartfelt words from a friend or family member. Cue the happy tears.

SEALING THE DEAL WITH VISUAL VOWS

THE MEANINGFUL SYMBOLIC ACT (or "MSA," as we like to call it) is another optional ceremonial addition that can take the teary-eyed, "they make me believe in love!" factor of your wedding to the next level. Unlike readings or vows, MSAs are visual: lighting a unity candle, sharing a goblet of wine (how medieval), and releasing butterflies or doves. Beyond those very traditional options, we encourage you to make up your own. Here are a few of our favorite ideas to get you started:

WINE LOCK BOX

This is a great "delayed gratification" act, where the couple write one another a love letter. During their ceremony, the bride and groom place the sealed letters in a lockbox with a bottle of wine and wine glasses. The box is locked until a specific anniversary (5 years works well), at which time the couple opens the box, enjoys the bottle, and reads their love letters. If this sounds like your thing, do some research and find a bottle that will peak around your chosen anniversary. For extra fun, use a hammer and nails to really seal that baby off, but make sure to get shatterproof stemware.

UNITY COCKTAIL

Pouring red and white wine together is almost too easy, and if you think about it, ease isn't really symbolic of marriage. In the Unity Cocktail, the bride and groom join together to mix a tasty drink. Choose a drink that's stirred for low volume, or use a cocktail shaker to wake your grandma up. If you see fit, select a drink that, when mixed, ends up being one of your wedding colors. If it's between color and flavor, however, choose flavor.

UMBRELLA CEREMONY

This Indonesian tradition signifies the way the new couple will need to weather the storms of life together. The couple take shelter under an umbrella while the officiant or a special guest pours a mixture of rice, coins, and candy to represent everlasting love, shared wealth, and the sweetness of marriage. For a little controlled chaos, invite any small children up to dig through the rice and loose change for candy.

REVERSE UNITY CANDLE

You know the traditional unity candle act, but if you want to keep your guests' attention, try the reverse unity candle. Every guest will need to take a candle when they arrive. After the couple light the unity candle, they take their candles to the wedding party, who also have candles. Each person lights the candle of the person next to them until everyone is holding a lit candle. In dry, outdoor climates, this could be risky, but if your venue is reasonably fireproof, this is a worthwhile variation on the original candle act.

PLANT A TREE

If you're not getting married in a place where you can just randomly plant a tree into the ground, make it a small tree and plant it in a nice pot. The bride and groom take turns filling the pot with soil, and each uses a separate watering can to water the roots. The important thing here is to understand how difficult it can be to keep a tree alive, and not put too much weight on whether the thing lives. A dead tree should not equal agony; at most, it should equal a fun couples trip to Home Depot on your one-month anniversary.

TIME CAPSULE

This is similar to the wine lockbox. Instead of booze and one never-read love letter, place saved mementos and notes you shared while you were dating into the time capsule. If guests wrote notes on their RSVPs, include those. Engagement photos are nice, too, or have someone snap a Polaroid and make it the last thing you place inside. Heck, throw in a bottle of wine or champagne if you'd like. Just like the lockbox, assign an opening date for the time capsule.

↑ *You probably shouldn't freestyle your vows, and you definitely should bring a written copy to the ceremony.*

How Other World Cultures Do This Wedding Thing

Wedding ceremonies are so culturally specific that you might get some serious déjà vu when you're planning your own. Looking to give your ceremony a unique feel? Look outside your culture. You may not want to incorporate all of the traditions below into your own ceremony, but you'll definitely enjoy learning about them.

PHILIPPINES
Releasing doves

This is exactly what it sounds like. The practice originated as a Filipino tradition, with the bride and groom releasing two doves representing peace and harmony in their marriage. This is all about logistics, and by making this part of your ceremony you're wagering that both doves will fly away, and that neither dove will shit on you. If everything works out, this will make for a pretty magical moment. Plus, one of your first acts as a married couple is helping caged birds escape! You're good people.

CONGO
Seriously, we're happy

Congolese couples (yes, "Congolese"—we checked) are considered serious about their marriage only if they keep a straight face for the entire wedding day, ceremony through reception. If they smile, it is assumed they do not understand the gravity of the vows they have taken. While a no-smile pact could make for a fun inside joke between you and your fiancé, it will no doubt be hard to maintain for your entire wedding day.

FRANCE
Wedding-day walk

In France, the groom meets the bride at her house on their wedding day, and together, they walk to the ceremony. And if their town is drawn by legendary Disney animators, small children block their path with white ribbons, and together the couple breaks through the symbolic barriers to arrive at the wedding. Weather and distance permitting, this sounds pretty special—even if you're the only ones who know the plan.

GREECE
Crowns for everyone

The best man, who actually leads the Greek Orthodox ceremony with the officiant, exchanges the wedding rings three times: groom to bride to groom, symbolizing the couple's balance of strengths and weaknesses. The best man then places crowns made of orange or gold blossoms on both the bride and groom. The crowns are connected by a ribbon, symbolizing unity. If your officiant can share the spotlight—and you're into crowns—this could be a great way to further personalize your ceremony.

KOREA
Beating the groom

Nothing says "we support you" like a group of guys beating your feet immediately following your wedding. In Korea, it's totally normal for the groom's friends to steal his shoes and tie his feet together before beating the soles of his feet with sticks and fish. And while they're doing this, they're quizzing the groom like a terrifying round of *Family Feud*. All of this is supposed to make the groom stronger before his wedding night. Fingers crossed that your grooms-men have never heard of this.

SPAIN
Brought to you by...

In Spain, the traditional wedding is paid for by godparents and sponsors, who are then recognized in various parts of the ceremony. If you're okay with your wedding being the matrimonial equivalent of a podcast, this is a pretty slick way to increase your open bar budget. These ceremonies also give brides and grooms their own mascots: the flower girl and ring bearer dress as tiny versions of the couple. The danger here is: these mini yous steal the show, and your guests demand a baby wedding.

SCOTLAND
Swords, pigs, and toddlers

There will be bagpipes. A Scottish wedding starts out sounding amazing: on the wedding day, the entire wedding party walks to the venue together throwing flower petals. If the party comes upon a funeral or a pig—so specific—it was an omen of bad luck, and they would go back and start their journey again. The groom wears a kilt, kilt jacket, and *sporran* (Gaelic for murse) in his clan's colors. The bride makes out like a bandit here, getting a sash in her new clan colors, an engraved teaspoon, and a family sword to give their firstborn son. If you're a lucky groom, the bride's family might give you a sword, too! The gravy on this mashed potato ceremony: A toddler (?) hands you a lucky horseshoe as you leave the ceremony. You, in turn, toss all the little children coins to collect. You'll need family colors, two swords, and a kilt, but otherwise we see no downside. Avoid porcine funerals.

SWEDEN
First!

As the bride and groom enter the church or venue together, the partner whose foot touches down across the entryway first is "the head of the household." Swedes are a generally fun-loving folk, and this is a playful tradition. The couple may time their steps to land at the same time, or maybe one partner will purposefully yield to the other. Even if there is disagreement at this point, there's still a shot at reclaiming the head of household. When the officiant asks "Will you marry him/her?" whoever says "*Ja!*" ("I do!") the loudest is the head of the household, no takesy-backsies. These kindergarten playground tactics are a great way to lighten up two rituals that are often a little stiff.

CHOOSING YOUR PROCESSIONAL MUSIC

SO MAYBE YOU'RE NOT INTO THE TRADITIONAL wedding march or think that Pachelbel's "Canon" is overplayed. Good news: We live in a time when almost anything could be considered processional music (the tunes that the wedding party walks down the aisle to). String quartet? Ethereal harpist? Your fave song of all time plus an excellent sound system? Only a few of the endless options to choose from—but which is best for your wedding? Take these five factors into consideration before spending hours debating 20 different flute versions of Beatles songs with your future spouse:

Walk—don't run—to it

Most couples choose a slower-tempo song for the procession, because slow walking looks stately and elegant. Faster songs mean speed walking, which potentially means your wedding party resembling a three-legged race at a family picnic. Another thing to consider: If there are any slow-moving elderly people or children in your ceremony, be sure to choose something they can keep up with as well (another argument against fast-paced songs).

Acoustics are important

If your venue is indoors, you already have more options, thanks to more forgiving room acoustics. Vocals can be harder to understand in outdoor settings, so consider using instrumental versions of your song choice if you're marrying al fresco (or just pick something well-known enough that people won't necessarily need to hear all the lyrics to "get it"). Some instruments like the harp or an acoustic guitar can also be harder to hear outdoors, so make sure your venue and sound system can handle whatever musical masterpiece you have in mind.

Make sure it's easy to cut off

You're probably not going to be able to get through your entire song (unless you have a gigantor wedding party), so select something that can easily fade out. If there's a specific part of the song that you want to play, work with the DJ/band to figure this out beforehand. Keep in mind that your wedding party might not move at exactly the same pace as you imagine (or as they do at the rehearsal dinner, for that matter), so leave a little wiggle room for the end point—how awkward would it be if your track ended before everyone made it to the altar? Yikes.

Get your venue and officiant's approval

Some religious ceremonies won't allow secular music. Some secular venues have limits on noise or space allotted for a band. Check all this out beforehand—after all that time spent searching for (read: arguing over) the perfect song with your partner, you wouldn't want to be shot down and have to go back to the drawing board for even more searching (arguing).

Decide whether you want to play a different song when your fiancé walks down the aisle

This is a great way to up the drama on your fiancé's entrance, but we wouldn't attempt a two-song processional if you have a small wedding party—you'll barely get through a snippet of the first song when you abruptly have to switch over for your partner's superstar moment. Other downside: You and your fiancé will have to choose two songs for the processional—which means even more hours spent over analyzing every song you've ever mildly liked.

Groom Service

TAKE A WALK ON THE WILD SIDE

Instead of simply walking down the aisle, some couples ask their wedding party to dance, shimmy, or sashay. Yes, this is your wedding, and yes, you should do whatever you want. But here's our 2 cents: Your ceremony is not a Broadway show or an episode of *Soul Train*. Any sort of choreographed routine runs the risk of looking forced—and is that really what you want for this spiritual moment in your life? All we ask is that you please think it through before asking your groomsmen to pop and lock down the aisle in front of everyone you know.

Reception

Besides love, it's the biggest reason why you're getting married.

The Fun Stuff

Lets face it: people go to weddings for the reception. Yes, they'll shed a happy tear or two at the ceremony—but ultimately, they'd prefer to celebrate you and your partner's love within the context of a dance floor, Top 40 playing, trying not to spill their cocktails as they attempt, only halfway successfully, to drop it low.

How do two mortals meet the impossible expectations contained in the word "reception"? If you feel overwhelmed, focus on the Holy Trinity of reception-planning: **food**, **drinks**, and **dancing**. Cover these bases, and your reception is more likely to be an incredible, life-affirming experience. This is a symbiotic relationship—if one is neglected, all fail.

"A party without cake
is just a meeting."

—JULIA CHILD

HOW A RECEPTION WORKS

LIKE SNOWFLAKES OR FINGERPRINTS, all wedding receptions are unique. But traditionally, some combination of the below happens. If you've been to even one wedding before, you already know all of this stuff and can probably skip this outline. Wedding newbs only beyond this point.

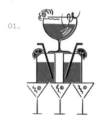

01.

COCKTAIL HOUR

After the ceremony, the wedding party leaves with the photographer to pose for pictures. That leaves the rest of the guests standing around awkwardly with nothing to do, hovering in a weird limbo between ceremony and reception. The solution: get them liquored up. Thus, the cocktail hour was born.

02.

ARRIVALS

The wedding party make their grand entrance to the reception. The newlyweds are introduced for the first time as a couple. It feels like something from a beauty pageant or a variety show from the 1960s. (Fair warning: you'll probably feel like that more than a few times during the reception.)

03.

DINNER

By this time, guests are probably pretty hungry and thinking, "Hey, where's the food?" Dinner is served—and it can be anything from a fine-dining feast, to an intimate family-style meal, to a catered Chipotle buffet. It's your call.

→ More on this in *What to Serve and How to Serve It*, page 90.

04.

TOASTS

The best man and maid of honor make their toasts—followed by the couple, their parents, and whoever else will be making a speech that night. There's a certain art to making a toast that has definitely not been mastered by every reception toast-maker out there—but don't worry, we'll help make yours a hit.

→ More on this in *Who Makes a Toast?*, page 96.

05.

FIRST DANCE

Your first dance as a married couple can be nerve-wracking; it's just the two of you on the dance floor for an entire song (three minutes go by very slowly when there's a room full of people staring at you). Just stay laser-focused on your new spouse— this can be a really special moment if you block out the audience.

06.

DANCING

Remember: the guests won't start dancing until you do. After the first dance, it's on you to ignite the dance party. Ask your wedding party to get on the dance floor the moment the first song starts. Shouldn't be too hard to convince them...

Continued on the next page

RECEPTION

07.

08.

09.

BOUQUET & GARTER TOSSES

Many people include these in their weddings, but they have pretty creepy meanings behind them if you really think about it (more on that later). Decide what's best for you, or make up your own traditions.

→ More on this in *Entertainment*, page 104.

CAKE CUTTING

About an hour before the end of the reception (right when guests are starting to lose some steam on the dance floor) is an excellent time to break out the cake and bring on the sugar rush.

LATE-NIGHT SNACK

Not everyone has a sweet tooth, so a lot of couples like to bring out other late-night snack options to keep their guests' bellies full and the party going. Think about foods that drunk people like (the greasier, the better) and, ideally, things that can be eaten on the dance floor (finger foods, anything on a stick, nothing too saucy).

10.

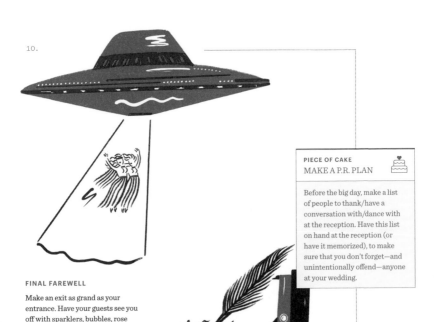

FINAL FAREWELL

Make an exit as grand as your entrance. Have your guests see you off with sparklers, bubbles, rose petals, or beach balls—or depart in a cool vintage car. The possibilities— and photo ops—are endless.

PIECE OF CAKE
MAKE A P.R. PLAN

Before the big day, make a list of people to thank/have a conversation with/dance with at the reception. Have this list on hand at the reception (or have it memorized), to make sure that you don't forget—and unintentionally offend—anyone at your wedding.

THE (SOMETIMES DISTURBING) MEANINGS BEHIND POPULAR RECEPTION TRADITIONS

MANY OF THE BELOVED TRADITIONS performed at wedding receptions today have been around for centuries. But, as we all know, the world was a very different place hundreds of years ago. Weddings are kind of like hot dogs: they're far more enjoyable if you don't know where they came from. But if you're curious, read on. You may never look at wedding receptions the same way again, but chances are you'll still like them (and hot dogs).

	ORIGIN	CREEPINESS (1 TO 10)
FIRST DANCE	This comes from the days of formal balls, where the first dance was led by guests of honor—visiting royalty or other distinguished, fancy types. At weddings, the guests of honor are obviously the couple, so they do the first dance.	**2** *Not creepy, besides the outdated class structures.*
THROWING A BOUQUET	In medieval times, having a piece of the bride's dress was considered lucky, so after the ceremony everyone would pounce and literally rip it off her body. This eventually evolved into throwing the bouquet—a less disturbing alternative.	**6** *The current tradition isn't creepy, but the original—the one that involves being clawed by wedding guests—is the stuff of nightmares.*
THE GARTER TOSS	This unsettling tradition also started centuries ago, when the bride and groom had to show proof of consummating the marriage. It was common to have family and friends in the room to witness the, uh, act. Since this is equal parts terrifying and invasive, eventually the groom just started tossing the garter out the door to prove that the deed was done. Now it's symbolically done at the wedding reception.	**10** *We don't even know where to start with this one.*

Continued on the next page

	ORIGIN	CREEPINESS (1 TO 10)
TIERED WEDDING CAKE	Like most of these traditions, the wedding cake also stems from medieval times, when it was customary for guests to bring small cakes to place in front of the bride and groom, who kissed over the pile for good luck. Today, tiered wedding cakes mimic that custom.	**0** *Total lack of creepy. It's actually pretty sweet (pun intended).*
CANS TIED TO THE GETAWAY CAR	In the English Tudor period, wedding guests would throw their shoes at the bride and groom's carriage because it was considered good luck if they hit the vehicle. Today, that would result in a lawsuit, so we tie shoes (or sometimes aluminum cans, because walking home barefoot is never fun) to the back of the car instead.	**2** *Not creepy, but completely reckless.*
GROOM'S CAKE	The groom's cake originated in Victorian England, when it was sliced and served to the bridesmaids at the end of the ceremony. It was said that if an unmarried woman slept with a slice of the cake under her pillow, she'd dream of her future husband.	**3** *Not very creepy, but certainly a waste of good cake.*
WEDDING FAVORS	Wedding favors date back to the 16th century, when European nobility handed out cubes of sugar—which was a delicacy at the time—to show off their wealth. As sugar became less expensive, sugar-coated almonds became the trend, usually packaged in bags of five representing health, wealth, happiness, fertility, and long life.	**1** *Not creepy, but trying to show off how much money you have is pretty tacky.*

Groom Service

PACIFIERS AND PAIN KILLERS

Your wedding is an all-ages event. You may want your reception to be an all-out rager, but remember: there will likely be children and elderly guests present. We're not suggesting you turn your party into a bingo parlor or a playground ball pit (but, in all honesty, both of those things would be amazing additions to a reception), but it's important to be cognizant of the varying age groups at the event.

Food

2

Food is the fuel that will power the party, but dinner is only the beginning. A well-designed menu primes your guests for a long night. Cake sweetens the deal with a sugar rush. The late-night snack inoculates against contagious yawns and balances the booze. You are now leaving the land of meat and potatoes.

"Eat what you like and let the food fight it out inside."

–MARK TWAIN

WHAT TO SERVE AND HOW TO SERVE IT

RECEPTION DINNERS HAVE BECOME MUCH more than a simple checkbox for "beef or chicken?" on the back of an RSVP card. These days, couples are serving everything from foie gras to chili dogs—there really is no wrong. When it comes to choosing what to serve at your reception, our advice is to make it personal: your favorite restaurant probably caters, as does your local hole-in-the-wall taco joint, or the place where you and your partner had your first date.

You also have a few options for how to serve the reception dinner. Below are the four most popular picks, ranked from most to least traditional. Choose whichever style suits your needs, budget, and desired formality level.

	TYPE	HOW IT WORKS	PROS	CONS
FORMAL ↑	**SIT-DOWN** *Budget: $$$$*	If you've seen a reception dinner in the movies, chances are it was a formal, sit-down affair. Guests are seated at assigned tables and are served a set menu by a waitstaff.	This is your most formal option, which also means that it's likely to make your wedding feel like a "special, once-in-a-lifetime occasion."	Assigned seating can be a bit of a hassle—especially when you have to worry about keeping apart divorced parents, exes, family rivals, and everyone away from your partner's handsy aunt.
	FAMILY-STYLE *Budget: $$*	Guests sit at long, Medieval Times-style tables. Food and dishes are placed in the center, and guests serve themselves. You can do assigned seats, or just let guests figure it out.	If you're going for warm, friendly, all-around chill vibes, nothing beats a good family-style meal.	With people serving themselves, you may run out of certain dishes quickly and have lots of leftovers with others.
	BUFFET *Budget: $*	We've all been to a buffet before—food is set up on tables and guests get up to serve themselves.	If having a formal dinner doesn't feel very "you," the buffet is a great alternative for a laid-back reception dinner. It's also a more budget-friendly option since it doesn't involve servers.	Guests could end up spending a long time waiting in line. And more time in line means less time on the dance floor.
CASUAL ↓	**FOOD TRUCK** *Budget: $$*	Hire your favorite local food truck to park outside your venue and service your guests' food needs all night long.	Food trucks can be lowbrow, but they also add a fantastic sense of novelty. Who doesn't love a good taco truck?	Again, guests will have to spend time waiting in line for their food instead of enjoying the party.

Rehearsal dinners are not actually about rehearsing.

Get the awkward hellos out of the way so your reception
can be an uninterrupted celebration.

After-Hours d'Oeuvres

It's important to keep the party going by serving snacks throughout the night. The later into the party (and the more intoxicated your guests), the greasier these snacks should be, satiating their drunk-person appetites and keeping them on the dance floor. Here are a few of our favorites, ranked from sober snacks to ultimate crunk cravings.

BLOOD ALCOHOL CONTENT		
.00	→ Fancy nuts → Popcorn → Cookies → Shrimp cocktail → Tater tots	
.04	→ Mac and cheese → DIY taco bar → Pizza → 10-foot sub sandwich → Mini doughnuts → Full-size doughnuts	
.08	→ Burgers and fries → DIY nacho bar → Chicken wings → Churros → Grilled cheese → Mini corn dogs	
.11	→ Jalapeño poppers → DIY hot dog bar → Frito pies → Philly cheesesteaks → Chicken and waffles → Catered Taco Bell	

3 **Drinks**

If food is the fuel to keep the party going, booze is the party itself. Not that drinking is the only way to have fun—it's certainly not—but when you're bringing together a large, diverse group of people who don't necessarily know each other, it can help cut the awkwardness and ignite the party. Which should always be your ultimate goal.

"I used to drink a lot. I still do, but I used to, too."

—MITCH HEDBERG

TWO WORDS: OPEN BAR

HAVING AN OPEN BAR AT YOUR WEDDING is essential, simply because so much of your party dreams (uninhibited dancing, poorly-matched romantic connections, and just general fun and laughs) will be amplified if your guests are liquored up. It is your duty as the host to make sure this happens by providing free drinks for everyone. If this doesn't sound like it's worth the cost for you, let us prove otherwise.

There's an Open Bar for Every Budget

Open bar doesn't necessarily mean providing every type of alcohol and letting your guests go at it. Curating your drink menu makes the whole evening easier: fewer drinks to choose from (or self-serve drinks) equals less time spent making drinks for the bartender, and hopefully less time spent waiting in line for guests—and it's easier on your wallet. The below ideas are not only surefire crowd-pleasers, they're budget-friendly, too (bonus!).

PRE-SELECTED COCKTAILS

Create a menu with two or three classic cocktails and a couple of wines or beers to choose from. Give the cocktails personalized handles like "The Newlywed" or "First Dance" to take the festivity level to 11.

PRE-MIXED SELF-SERVE DRINKS*

Serve pre-mixed drinks from punch bowls or water coolers that are constantly being refilled. Senior prom vibes in the best way.

SELF-SERVE BEERS ON TAP

Having a serve-yourself beer on tap station (or, if you're really looking to get nostalgic, a keg) gives guests the satisfaction of being their own bartender.

*If you're considering doing a self-serve bar, be sure to appoint someone to refill the alcohol and glasses, and—most importantly—keep the area tidy throughout the night. A self-serve station can quickly become a disaster zone if left unattended.

Still not sure if you should go with the open-bar option or not? We made a handy flowchart:

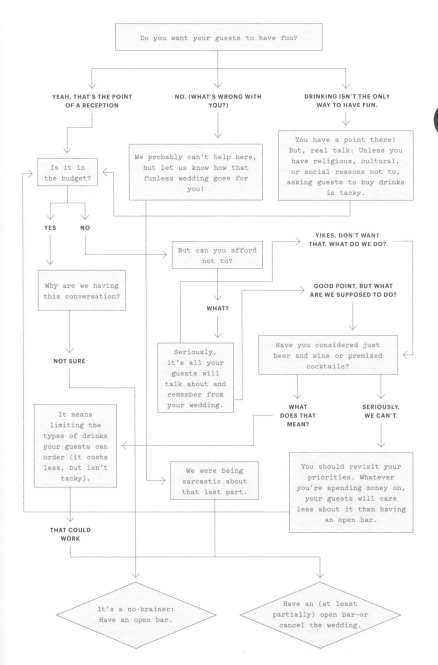

Beyond the Open Bar

If you're doing open bar, you're doing well. However, should you have the desire to go above-and-beyond the call of duty, here are a few ideas to help you accomplish that goal.

DIY

→ Make-your-own margarita bar
→ Adult snow cone stand
→ Self-serve beers on tap

DELIGHTFULLY IRONIC

→ Jell-O shots
→ Punch bowls
→ Keg
→ Bucket of ice filled with bottled beers

THOUGHTFUL

Hangover Helper Gift Bags:
→ Aspirin
→ Gatorade
→ Fast food gift cards
→ Custom "Do not disturb: Recovering from Jack & Jane's wedding" hotel door-hangers

CLASSY

→ Wine, whiskey, or beer tastings

Groom Service
WHO MAKES A TOAST?

Best man

Maid of honor

You and your partner*

Your parents

Your partner's parents

Your aunt, after a few too many glasses of champagne**

*Toasting brings everyone together for the warm and fuzzies, but it's also very important because it gives you a chance to thank everyone for attending/ being in your wedding, and your parents (or whomever) for hosting it. This is crucial, because once the party gets going, it's going to be hard for you to thank every single guest personally. And besides, who doesn't appreciate a good public shout-out?

**This one is not so much a "should," as a "prepare yourself, because it will happen."

Music & Dancing

Trust us: Music choice can make or break a reception. Play the right tunes at your wedding, and you'll have to forcefully remove guests from your party. On the other hand, clearing the dance floor is as easy as Y-M-C-A.

"If people stand in a circle long enough, they'll eventually begin to dance."

—GEORGE CARLIN

HUMANS VS. MACHINES

WHICH APPROACH BETTER SUITS YOUR TASTE, desired party vibe, and those killer dance moves you've been waiting to bust out? Here's the breakdown.

TYPE	PROS	CONS
LIVE BAND	**IT'S AN "EVENT":** In the "unforgettable experiences" department, physical instruments and musicians trump a guy with a laptop any day.	**IT'S EXPENSIVE:** Booking live talent is not cheap. If you want a live show in your honor, you'll have to pay for it.
DJ	**YOU'LL GET A GREATER VARIETY OF MUSIC:** Bands are like restaurant menus—if they're offering 50 pages worth of options, chances are all of it will be mediocre and may even make you sick. DJs, on the other hand, have all the greats right at their fingertips. **IT'S CHEAPER:** Cost is obviously the biggest advantage of hiring a DJ, especially if you hire your friend (and we all have a friend who's a DJ... or at least a "DJ"). **IT'S LESS COMPLICATED:** A string quartet or a Jimi Hendrix cover band needs more space and power supply than a DJ — which may open up your venue options.	**EVERYONE'S A DJ:** As we mentioned, everyone knows a DJ... or 10. The title's thrown around pretty loosely these days, which means there's a higher risk of accidentally hiring a total vibe-killer. Screen potential talent very carefully.

PIECE OF CAKE
TAKE SONG REQUESTS BY MAIL

When sending out your RSVP cards, include a space for your guests to write in a song request. After you get all of the cards back, compile the requests into a playlist and give it to the DJ ahead of time.

WE CAN DANCE IF WE WANT TO

YOU PROBABLY SHOULDN'T DO A CHOREOGRAPHED DANCE at your wedding. Unless you and your partner are members of the New York City Ballet or competitive tango dancers, you risk looking like a bad episode of *Dancing with the Stars*. But either way, the first dance is the first public statement you and your partner will make about who you are as a married couple. Song choice and style reveal a lot about a couple's identity, so choose wisely and consider the advice below.

Choosing A Song You Won't Regret

The perfect first dance song should live in a sweet spot between the following three categories.

QUESTIONS TO ASK YOURSELF:

MEANINGFUL TO YOU AND YOUR PARTNER

→ What song was playing when we met?

→ What's the first song we danced to?

→ What's the first song we made out to?

→ Do we have a mutual favorite song?

→ Is there a song that perfectly describes our relationship?

APPROPRIATE FOR THE EVENT

→ Is the song we've chosen too long (anything over three and a half minutes)?

→ Is it inappropriate for the audience (gangster rap)?

→ Is it actually a breakup song ("Love Will Tear Us Apart")?

→ Is it too weird to dance to (anything classified as "experimental")?

NOT A CLICHÉ

→ Please, for the love of God, no more Etta James.

First Dancing With the Stars

Take inspiration from these glitter-covered humans' first dances as married glitter-covered humans. Some are oldies, some are new tunes, and some songs were recorded by the couple (probably shy away from that last example).

WHO DANCED TO IT	SONG	ARTIST
George Clooney and Amal Alamuddin	"Why Shouldn't I?" by Cole Porter	Performed by Nora Segal
Justin Timberlake and Jessica Biel	"A Song for You"	Donny Hathaway
Jennifer Aniston and Justin Theroux	"Chandelier"	Sia
Kim Kardashian and Kanye West, Gene Simmons and Shannon Tweed, Nicole Kidman and Keith Urban, Chelsea Clinton and Marc Mezvinsky	"At Last"	Etta James
Reese Witherspoon and Jim Toth	"Make You Feel My Love"	Bob Dylan
Neil Patrick Harris and David Burtka	"A Moment Like This"	Kelly Clarkson
Christina Hendricks and Geoffrey Arend	"Origin of Love"	From *Hedwig and the Angry Inch*
President Barack Obama and Michelle Robinson	"You and I"	Stevie Wonder
Beyoncé and Jay-Z	"Crazy in Love"	Beyoncé featuring Jay-Z
Ellen DeGeneres and Portia de Rossi	"Ribbon in the Sky"	Stevie Wonder
Fergie and Josh Duhamel	"Sweethearts Together"	The Rolling Stones
David Beckham and Victoria Adams	"It Had to Be You"	The Starlight Orchestra
Billy Joel and Katie Lee	"Moon River"	Audrey Hepburn
Tom Cruise and Katie Holmes	"Songbird"	Fleetwood Mac
Mark Zuckerberg and Priscilla Chan	"Last Night on Earth"	Green Day
Paul McCartney and Nancy Shevell	"My Valentine"	Paul McCartney
Kate Middleton and Prince William	"Your Song" by Elton John	Performed by Ellie Goulding

WHAT MAKES A GOOD MIX?

MAYBE YOU GIVE THIS TO THE DJ, or maybe you opt to DJ the party yourself with nothing but a playlist on your phone. When making your own mix, remember: Your ultimate goal is to get (and keep) as many people as possible on the dance floor. Your playlist should please a wide range of guests, from pretentious twentysomethings to awkwardly shimmying moms.

THE IDEAL MIX IS:

→ Uptempo

→ Danceable

→ Full of crowd pleasers (like Motown and MJ)

→ Peppered with a few Top 40 hits for good measure

Classic Songs: Know When to Fold 'Em

There are some songs everyone knows, and that can lead to uncomfortable dancing, sing-alongs, and sloppy choreography. Just because you've heard them at every other reception doesn't mean you have to make room for these songs on your playlist. Keep the ones you love, say goodbye to the songs that have overstayed their welcome, and make the DJ a "do not play" list for the songs you can't stand ("Margaritaville," anyone?).

SONG	PARTY NOTES
"Cupid Shuffle" by Cupid (or "Cha Cha Slide" by DJ Casper)	In terms of bodies on the dance floor, these songs are going to get you quantity, not quality. Even if this is the one dance everyone at your reception does, it's impossible to mess up the moves.
"Shout" by The Isley Brothers (or "Twist and Shout" by The Beatles)	Do you want your Ferris Bueller moment, or do you want all of your guests on their feet? There is no shame in choosing Beatles over Brothers—just don't lip sync "Danke Schoen" right before.
"The Train (C'mon N' Ride It)" by Quad City DJ's (or "Love Train" by The O'Jays)	Because "train" is in the title, a human serpent will form on the dance floor and snake its way around your reception venue. Lots of sweaty bodies, lots of hands. But as the groom you'll probably be the conductor, so that's fun.

Continued on the next page

RECEPTION

SONG	PARTY NOTES
"Baby Got Back" by Sir Mix-a-Lot (or "Ice Ice Baby" by Vanilla Ice)	We could never fully endorse a song that objectifies the female body like Mix-A-Lot's most famous tune. Better to opt for the irony of Vanilla Ice.
"Thriller" by Michael Jackson	You'll have one person who knows the shimmy-clap, and half will know the monster claws, but nobody knows the whole "Thriller" dance. It's an infectious song even without the choreography, but why not pull something less obvious from MJ's incredible catalogue? Recommended: "P.Y.T."
"Your Love" by The Outfield (or "Don't Stop Believing" by Journey)	These songs are all about the intro sing-along. They're not easy to dance to at all.
"Pour Some Sugar on Me" by Def Leppard (or "You Shook Me All Night Long" by AC/DC)	Just in case you wanted to see your parents, aunts, and uncles grinding.
"White Wedding" (or "Mony Mony") by Billy Idol	We get it: Billy says "wedding." Isn't this just a lot of air guitar, though? "Mony" is a better choice for dancing.
"Y.M.C.A." by Village People (or "It's Raining Men" by The Weather Girls)	These are great for when you want to see any of your super conservative family members dancing to a gay anthem.
"Celebration" by Kool & The Gang (or "September" by Earth, Wind & Fire)	A song about a celebration at a celebration: so meta. For your upbeat '70s Soul, we're more into "September" by EWF. They're singing about a great memory and dancing, which is slightly less obviously meta.
"Love Shack" by The B-52s (or "Girls Just Wanna Have Fun" by Cyndi Lauper)	These '80s hits are what a rainbow sounds like. Rainbows are about refracted light and promises, which is also the essence of a wedding reception.
"Sweet Caroline" by Neil Diamond (or "Jessie's Girl" by Rick Springfield)	A pair of awesome songs, no doubt. But what do you do between the choruses? You're likely to lose some novice dancers with these, but it's worth it.
"Wild Thing" (or "Funky Cold Medina") by Tone Loc	The hip-hop equivalent of "Pour Some Sugar On Me." However, if you've ever sampled the chewy, cheesy menu at Delicious Pizza in L.A., you'll be thinking of their Slaughtahouse slices and Funky Cold Sangria for 4 tasty minutes. Yes, please.
"I Will Survive" by Gloria Gaynor (or "Respect" by Aretha Franklin)	Every man, woman, and child wishes they could sing like these female powerhouses. These are sing-along songs we wholethroatedly endorse.
"Brown-Eyed Girl" (or "Wild Night") by Van Morrison	There's nothing wrong with "Brown-Eyed Girl," but "Wild Night" is not only the superior dance song, but it may be the quintessential summer song.
"Macarena" by Los del Rio	Like, just don't.

Groom Service

KEEP DANCES WITH PARENTS SHORT

This can be touching, but it can also get real weird real fast if you think about it too hard. If you decide to do parent dances, keep them short and sweet. Remember: The more time you spend on these dances, the less time your guests will have on the dance floor.

Entertainment

5

"It ain't no fun if the
homies can't have
none."

—SNOOP DOGG

Why stop at the Holy Trinity of food, drinks,
and dancing when you can push your reception
even further, achieving party nirvana? These
finishing touches will take your reception to
the next level—and make guests remember it
for years to come.

BE THE HOST WITH THE MOST

LOOKING FOR WAYS TO TAKE YOUR RECEPTION FROM "Eh, pretty good," to "Holy shit! Best reception ever!!!!"? Well, consider these the cherries atop your delicious reception sundae. Now dig in.

TAROT CARD READER

Let your guests find out what their futures hold. This is something unique that most people find fun (or at least funny) and would secretly like to try, but wouldn't necessarily pay for themselves.

TABLE GAMES

Create your own personalized mad libs, crossword puzzles, or word searches, and put them on the tables or bar to keep guests entertained throughout the night.

MESSAGE IN A BOTTLE

Guests write notes to you and the bride on little pieces of paper and then put them in a glass bottle to be opened on your one-year anniversary.

"CLASS PICTURE"

Toward the end of the reception, ask all of your guests to line up (tall people in the back!) for a throwback "class picture," just like elementary school. Yes, this will be hard with a large group, but that's half the fun.

BUTCHER PAPER AND CRAYONS AT THE BAR

Who doesn't want to relive the days when drawing on the table with Crayolas was socially acceptable?

BRIDE & GROOM PORTRAIT GALLERY

When sending your RSVP cards, ask guests to draw a picture of you and your partner on the back. Collect the portraits and display them in a gallery at the reception—the different levels of artistic talent will be entertaining.

KARAOKE ROOM

Discover which guests have a diva streak or lost dreams of becoming a rockstar. Seedy karaoke bars also make great after-party destinations.

Continued on the next page

RECEPTION

VIDEO BOOTH

Instead of a photo booth, have a station where guests can record short, personal video dedications to you and your partner. You can have the highlights edited into a longer keepsake video afterward.

TELEPHONE WHERE GUESTS CAN LEAVE A MESSAGE

Set up a vintage rotary telephone station—or, better yet, a phone booth—where guests can leave messages for you and your partner. The messages will get better as the night goes on (and your guests get drunker).

NEWLYWEDS TRAVEL MAP

Ask guests to write about their favorite destination in a giant atlas. The couple tries to visit one place every year.

LOUNGE AREA

Create a "chill zone" with comfortable places to sit, snacks, and games where people can take a break from dancing throughout the night. Maybe even a fire pit and s'mores, if possible?

"If it's boring, then it's tiring."

—JACKIE COOPER

ENCOURAGE GUESTS TO PASS NOTES DURING DINNER

Break all the etiquette rules. Leave paper and pens on guests' tables, with words of encouragement for them to pass notes to each other (or you and your partner) during the dinner hour.

CARD GAMES, DICE GAMES

Leave packs of cards or dice on the table as favors for guest to play with both during and after the reception. Personalize the packaging, and include a note that encourages guests to partake in some light gambling.

NEWLYWED SHOE GAME

Place two chairs back-to-back on the dance floor for you and your partner. Remove both of your shoes, then trade a shoe with your new spouse so that you're holding one of each. Have guests ask a series of questions about your relationship (i.e. "Who will do most of the cooking?" "Who said 'I love you' first?"). After each question, hold up the shoe of the person you think is the answer to the question.

COMMEMORATIVE POSTER

Instead of your run-of-the-mill guest book, have a custom poster designed for your big day. Guests sign the poster, and you have a beautiful art piece to frame and hang in your house for years to come.

LAWN GAMES

Make your favorite lawn games into a tournament (if you don't have an outdoor area at your venue, just play on the dance floor). Have prizes for the winners of each round.

POLAROID BOOK

Guests take Polaroids throughout the night and attach them in a book with a note or a fun memory they've had with you and your new spouse. Talk about a great takeaway.

PICTIONARY TOURNAMENT

It's a classic party game for a reason—everyone loves it. Divide guests up into teams and give the winners a special prize.

CIGAR BAR

Set up a table with a bunch of different types of cigars for guests to choose from. The ultimate bonding experience.

WEDDING BINGO

Have each guest write a "little-known fact" about themselves on their RSVP card. Make those responses into bingo cards—the first guest to get "bingo" from matching facts to guests gets a prize.

FISHBOWL

Write dares on little pieces of paper, and place them in a fishbowl at you and your partner's table. Guests must draw and complete a dare to get you both to kiss.

PIÑATA

The couple (that's you) gets to go first. If you don't succeed, open it up to the wedding party. Fill it with something unexpected, but make sure it won't injure anyone as it falls out. Maybe don't fill it with, you know, bees.

CLONE YOURSELF

Receptions are busy, and you're going to feel like you've been spread too thin by the end of the night. Combat this by going even thinner—get cardboard cutouts made of you and your partner, and pass yourselves around at your reception for photo ops and relatives with poor vision.

PINBALL MACHINES

Old-school pinball machines are so cool, and are available for rent. But beware: you may have trouble getting rid of the line of addicted arcade nerds gathered around it once the party's over.

RECEPTION

Weddings Without Borders

Love knows no bounds, but getting married is vastly different depending on where you are in the world. These may not all be traditions that you'd want to incorporate into your own wedding reception, but if you're anything like us, you'll just enjoy knowing that they exist somewhere on Earth.

LATIN AMERICA: GO CRAZY

Many Latin American weddings celebrate the *hora loca*—the transition between the last hour of the reception and the after party. Carnival-esque dancers come out and perform, and surprise costumes (hats, sunglasses, boas, noisemakers) are hidden underneath each table for guests to wear—and aren't revealed until the craziness begins. The goal is to get everyone all riled up to keep the party going for even longer.

MEXICO: WEAR YOUR HEART—AND CASH—ON YOUR SLEEVE

Money dances with the bride are common in many cultures, but one thing that's cool about Mexico's version is that the groom can get in on the action, too. Relatives take turns dancing with both the bride and groom and pinning money to their clothes, giving the couple a chance to spend quality time with each of their guests, and letting them make some cash for that honeymoon fund.

SWEDEN: SHARE THE LOVE

Swedes are known for their progressive views on sex. This extends to their weddings, where if the groom leaves the room for any reason, all of the other men at the wedding are allowed to steal a kiss from the bride. Same goes for the groom and female guests if the bride leaves the room—equal rights. Sounds like our parents in the '60s, man.

NORWAY: HAVE YOUR CAKE AND DRINK IT, TOO

Norwegian weddings serve a cake called a *kransekake*, made from donut-like almond cake rings that form a cone shape. A bottle of wine is placed in the center, slowly revealed as the guests eat the cake around it.

VENEZUELA: ADIOS, AMIGOS!

Everyone's heard of an Irish exit, but what about a Venezuelan exit? It's good luck for Venezuelan newlyweds to sneak away before the reception is over without getting caught. It's also good luck for whichever guest first discovers that they're gone. Prepare to feel like you're a teenager again, sneaking out your bedroom window to go make out in your car.

GERMANY: EMBRACE YOUR INNER LUMBERJACK

Ever want to feel like you're on one of those newlywed game shows, where couples put their relationship to the test while embarrassing themselves before a live studio audience? Just attend a German wedding, where the bride and groom have to work together to saw a large log in half in front of all their wedding guests. The act symbolizes the obstacles they will have to overcome in marriage. (Rugged and romantic!)

FRANCE: BE A POTTY MOUTH

French weddings often serve a *croquembouche*, a literal tower of cream puffs that's incredibly delicious. Then there's *La Soupe*, which is made from delicious French chocolates—but served out of a (new) toilet bowl that the bride and groom have to eat from for good luck. If that sounds nauseating to you, consider this: at least they no longer make *La Soupe* out of random reception dinner leftovers and trash, like they did back in the day.

Tuxes in the Wild

The reception may be over, but the party's just begun. Where will you take your tux after hours? Below are a few ideas.

→ Burger joint
→ Dive bar
→ 24-hour diner
→ Karaoke spot
→ Hotel lobby
→ Drug store beer run
→ Bowling alley

Groom Service

TAKE A TIMEOUT FOR TWO

It's easy to get caught up in the excitement of the party, but be sure
to steal a moment alone with your partner sometime during or right
after the reception. It's important for the two of you to revel in the
utter coolness of what you just did—you're a married couple now!
Bring on the new life phase.

Style Guide

Dressing formally is not an everyday occurrence. Suits and tuxedos are reserved for a handful of special occasions (weddings, proms, and red carpet events—if you're some sort of bigwig or reality TV star), so most guys don't have a ton of experience wearing them. Which also means that knowing how, what, and when to wear them can get very confusing. If you can barely spell "cummerbund"—let alone know how to wear one— fear not; we'll break it down in this section. Because dressing up should mean looking and feeling like the best version of yourself, not like an awkward version of yourself in a costume.

A TUXEDO IS NOT A COSTUME; IT'S A SUIT OF ARMOR

WHAT SHOULD I WEAR?

TUXEDOS (PG. 149) are more formal than **SUITS** (PG. 175). You probably already knew this, and if you didn't— where have you been? But while you're well aware that the tuxedo is the suit's older and more sophisticated cousin, you may not know exactly what distinguishes the two from each other. Here's the breakdown:

NOTCH LAPEL TUXEDO

Unlike suits, tuxedos have satin lapels, as well as satin stripes down the sides of the pants.

Tuxedos are traditionally worn with **BOW TIES** (PG. 140), while suits are worn with **NECKTIES** (PG. 139)—but in this day and age, the rules are loosening up, and your neck-embellishment options have become a little more interchangeable.

A tuxedo worn with a bow tie calls for a formal tuxedo shirt with a **WING TIP COLLAR** (PG. 130). You'd never wear a wing tip collar with a suit—even if you chose to wear a bow tie, you'd wear it with a regular spread collar.

WING TIP SHIRT

BLACK LEATHER SHOES

Your **SHOE** (PG. 136) options for suits are pretty much endless—oxfords, slippers, loafers—while tuxedos are traditionally worn with black patent oxfords. Again, *rules are (sometimes) meant to be broken*, and today's men are branching out more with their footwear, even if they opt for a tuxedo. Do you.

So should you wear a tuxedo or a suit to your event? Only you can answer that question. Look deep inside yourself, meditate, wander off into the desert on a spiritual quest for which formalwear best calls to your soul. Or, you know, just take a look at the event, its **DRESS CODE** (PG. 120) (if there is one), and what the other attendees are wearing—and follow accordingly.

If you're a groom and your bride is wearing a princess gown in your wedding, you may look too casual standing next to her in a suit. Go for a tux. Conversely, if you're having a sunset beach wedding and the bride's in a flowy, less-traditional dress, you'll probably look like a buttoned-up fool in a black tuxedo. Go for a suit. These are just things to consider. *In the end, it's your wedding and you can wear whatever you want*—as long as it's not a tuxedo with flip-flops.

PLEASE DON'T WEAR A TUXEDO WITH FLIP-FLOPS.

PICK YOUR DRESS CODE

Before anxiety kicks in, because *how do I choose*, remember that your guests will probably be more concerned with what they're wearing than what you're wearing. Choosing the right dress code carries a little more weight, as it can define the vibe of your wedding. If you know your venue and ceremony time, keep those factors in mind.

CASUAL (1)(2)(3)(4)(5) **FORMAL**

On the next few pages, you'll find our simple formality scale to help you choose a fitting dress code (pun intended, 100%). The spectrum runs from the informal (1) (street clothes) to the formal (5) (first-class passenger on the Titanic).

Now, let's figure out what each code means to you. The rules may seem strict (and the really formal ones are) but, as you might have noticed, we want you to use our guidelines in whatever way best serves your wedding. So if you really want glitter, you can now tell your partner we said that was sort of okay. (No we didn't.)

THINKING OF SKIPPING THE DRESS CODE? Maybe you feel like asking all your guests to dress a particular way—or forcing them to rent a tux—is too demanding. Do this: Think of the last wedding you went to that had no dress code. Was there a guy wearing something ridiculous? That guy could have used a dress code.

WHITE TIE	BLACK TIE
Formality: ⑤	*Formality:* ④

ALSO KNOWN AS: Full Dress, Formal	**ALSO KNOWN AS:** Semi-formal

ALSO KNOWN AS: Full Dress, Formal

- White bow tie
- White waistcoat
- White wing-tip tuxedo shirt
- Button studs and cufflinks
- Tailcoat with black pleated tuxedo pants
- Black patent-leather shoes and black socks

White tie is reserved for diplomatic galas, extremely formal ceremonies, and royal weddings. It is the most strict of dress codes, so stick to the list. The "waistcoat" and "tailcoat" are mysteries to most. A waistcoat is essentially a vest with lapels. A tailcoat is a short jacket with peak lapels and long tails, designed to be left open. Proportions are everything, so you'll need high-waisted pants so the waistcoat covers your pant waist without dropping below the short front of the tailcoat. We'll wait here while you read that again.

ALSO KNOWN AS: Semi-formal

- Black bow tie
- White tuxedo shirt
- Button studs and cufflinks
- White pocket square
- Black or Midnight Blue single-button tuxedo
- Black patent-leather shoes and black socks

Black tie is a common dress code for formal weddings, company awards nights, charity events, or formal holiday parties. Black tie is nearly as strict as white tie, in that visual personality is not encouraged. You do get to select from two lapel styles and two tuxedo colors. You can also wear a more contemporary tuxedo shirt with a fold-down collar. If you need suspenders, match them to your tuxedo. A low-cut vest—matched to your tuxedo—or a black cummerbund is also optional.

CREATIVE BLACK TIE

Formality: ④

ALSO KNOWN AS: Festive

- Black bow tie
- White tuxedo shirt
- Button studs and cufflinks
- White pocket square
- Black or midnight blue single-button tuxedo
- Black patent leather shoes and black socks
- One interesting thing

The Oscars, the Emmys, and especially the Tonys, are a great place to find examples of creative black tie. Largely created by "the industry" in the '90s, this code allows for individuality while observing most of the black tie requirements. Have fun choosing your jacket, shoes, tie, pocket square, or shirt, but deviate from the traditional in only one category. For example, if your jacket is blue velvet, wear black patent leather shoes, a white dress shirt, and a black necktie or bow tie. Anything more? Proceed with caution (and finesse).

BLACK TIE OPTIONAL

Formality: ③

ALSO KNOWN AS: Informal
RELATED TO: Lounge, business formal

- White dress shirt
- Cufflinks
- White pocket square
- Navy or charcoal suit
- Black leather dress shoes and black socks

Black-tie optional is on the very edge of high formality. This dress code is considerate and inclusive of guests who may not own a tuxedo. If possible, guests wear a tuxedo and follow the black tie rules. Next best thing? A dark suit with black leather dress shoes, a solid necktie or bow tie, and a white dress shirt. This combination also works well as business formal, sometimes simply called "business." Skip the belt and wear cufflinks to elevate your look.

COCKTAIL ATTIRE

Formality: ②

ALSO KNOWN AS: Business casual

- Necktie or bow tie
- White, blue, or pink dress shirt
- Navy, blue, brown, grey or charcoal suit
- Black or brown dress shoes
- Black or brown dress socks

Cocktail attire or business casual require a formal suit, though none require a tuxedo. Take liberties with your suit color—navy, blue, brown, grey, or charcoal—and you may now wear notch lapels. Brown shoes are also on the menu, and they don't necessarily need to be high-polished. Shirt options now include pastel blue and pink. Also fair game: neckties and bow ties with subtle patterns, lapel pins, patterned pocket squares, and tie bars.

CASUAL DRESS

Formality: ①

ALSO KNOWN AS: Smart casual

- Collared dress shirt
- Blazer
- Dress pants or chinos
- Dress shoes with interesting socks

As with all dress codes, err on the side of formality: no polo shirts, denim, shorts, or sandals.

A patterned jacket with contrasting dress pants or chinos, or patterned pants with a solid contrast blazer work well. Or try a patterned dress shirt without a tie with a matching suit. In this case, an interesting pair of socks— or no socks at all—would be a great way to display personality without going overboard. Ties are optional.

HOW TO SPOT A
QUALITY GARMENT

CONSTRUCTION

The first sign of a good quality suit is the construction. Full canvassing is the highest level of suit construction. A full canvassed suit has horse hair stitched into the inner lining of the suit jacket, extending down the entire front length of the jacket. It allows the wearer's body to mold to the suit, creating a shape that drapes naturally and looks sharp.

FABRIC

Quality suits will be made using natural materials—most commonly wool, cotton, linen, and silk. Suits that are made using synthetic materials like polyester will be far less durable, won't breathe well, and will have a shiny appearance. A quality suit will also have extra fabric sewn to the major seams so that alterations can be made if the wearer were to gain or lose weight.

BUTTONS

The buttons of a quality suit will be made from horn and not plastic. Quality buttons are thick and sturdy and well stitched to the fabric. The buttons on the suit's jacket sleeve near the wrist will be working buttons meaning that they can actually be unbuttoned and the sleeve can be rolled up your wrist.

PICK STITCHING

Lapels should have more noticeable stitching than what you would find on cheap off the rack suits. Pick stitching is done by hand, as opposed to machine stitching, and is one of the clear signs of a good-quality suit.

THE NITTY-GRITTY OF TUXEDOS

Now that you've studied up on the basic differences between a tuxedo and a suit, as well as the often-confusing world of formal dress codes, we can move on to the fun stuff. Right now, you may be asking yourself, "What on Earth could be fun about dressing up in a stuffy old penguin suit that looks just like every other penguin suit out there?" Trust us: It can be fun, and it doesn't have to. In the following pages, we'll get into the details—**LAPEL SHAPES** (PG. 126), **TIE OPTIONS** (PG. 139), **SHOE CHOICE** (PG. 136), **SHIRT COLORS** (PG. 129) and more—that will personalize your suit or tux, and pull your entire look together. If you're confused about when to wear a shawl-collar jacket, or you want to experiment with pocket squares but are nervous about looking contrived—don't worry, we've got you. Consider this your how-to guide in taking your wedding look to the next level.

Lapel Choice

Which lapels are appropriate for your event, and what your
lapel says about you.

NOTCH LAPEL

The standard in men's suiting today, notch
lapels are found on everything from sport
coats to business suits. They have a "notch"
where the jacket collar meets the lapel, and
are extremely versatile—when in doubt, make
it a notch lapel suit. *That being said, notch
lapels are considered more casual than other
lapel types, so avoid wearing them at the most
formal black-tie events or all those red-carpet
affairs you attend.*

PEAK LAPEL

Peak lapels are slightly wider than notch
lapels, with edges that "peak" upward toward
your face. Originally seen in highly formal,
highly traditional garments like tailcoats, the
peak lapel has since made its way into tuxedo
and suit jackets alike. *It's generally viewed as
more formal than the notch lapel, and, because
it's less common, more of a statement.* But
don't shy away—because they point upward,
peak lapels have the effect of making you look
taller and slimmer. Win-win.

SHAWL COLLAR

Shawls aren't just for little old ladies. Shawls
(collars, that is) are characterized by a
modern, rounded shape, and are primarily
seen on tuxedos and dinner jackets. *While
shawl lapels are pretty much only found on
black tie-appropriate garments, some would
argue that they are less formal than a peak
lapel.* You could also argue they have more
panache. Use your judgment based on the
event and your personal style.

Single vs. Double Breasted

Yes, double-breasted suits and tuxedos are back, and yes, you can wear them anywhere.

Single-breasted

Double-breasted

Double-breasted suit jackets have overlapping front flaps and two sets of buttons. Traditionally associated with everything from '30s gangsters to '80s Wall Street brokers, today's double-breasted suits are a slimmer cut (which makes them much more flattering), and perfect for the guy who wants a bold look. *While viewed as more formal than its single-breasted brother, we say wear the DB wherever you want:* wedding, event, office, burger joint— it's just that classic-cool.

Material

The material quality of your suit and accessories affects the look and fit of your entire outfit.

WOOL

The most popular fabric for formal suits and tuxedos, wool drapes beautifully and has a sleek finish that makes it look more "polished." It's also known to be both insulating and breathable, basically making it the do-it-all renaissance man of the suiting world. It's hard to go wrong with wool.

SILK

Silk looks and feels delicate, but it's actually the strongest natural fiber—a good quality for accessories like ties and pocket squares that are constantly pulled, knotted, and folded. Silk has a natural elasticity that keeps wrinkles out, and a heft that provides a nice drape. While other materials are sometimes considered seasonal, silk is considered a year-round fabric.

COTTON

Cotton is breathable, making it perfect for dress shirts. Some manufacturers use polyester to cut costs, adding durability and wrinkle resistance, but poly reduces breathability. What does that mean for you? Shirts that get very, very sweaty. You might spend three minutes ironing a cotton shirt, but at least it's not a biohazard. Cotton is also great for pocket squares and ties, adding crisp textural variety against a wool jacket.

Color

It's not all black or white. Sometimes it's blue, pink, stripes, plaid, or prints. While *white shirts are best for formal events*—white tie, black tie, or black tie optional dress codes—blue or pink shirts are business casual classics. Other colors or prints can be mixed in depending on the event and dress code, but they're traditionally viewed as casual styles.

Collar

The sheer number of collar options in this world is staggering. Here's a breakdown of the ones you're most likely to encounter.

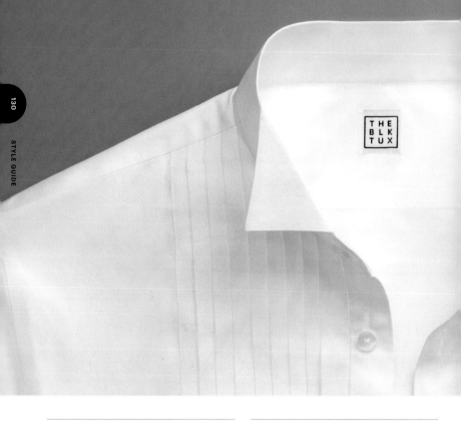

SPREAD COLLAR

This is the most common type of collar, and the most versatile. Spread collars come in a variety of points and angles, from forward point collars with a narrow spread, to cutaway collars with a wide spread (the "spread" refers to the distance between the collar points). It's kind of your do-it-all shirt style.

WING TIP COLLAR

The most formal collar option, the wing tip gets its name from the fold-out collar points that look like wings. It's designed to be worn with a bow tie and tuxedo—wear it tieless and casual, and you'll definitely get a few confused stares.

BUTTON DOWN COLLAR

Originally seen only on Oxford button-down shirts, this sporty collar has since made its way into more casual shirting. It can be worn with or without a tie, but is a definite "no" at formal events.

CLUB COLLAR

Originating at English boarding schools in the 1930s, the Club collar and its rounded edges have experienced a recent resurgence. More casual in style, it can be worn without a tie.

Bib

Why does my shirt have more shirt on top of it?

Some dress shirts have a rectangular panel that runs up the front of the shirt.
It's called a "bib," and it's much more sophisticated than what a baby
wears while eating mushy peas: it doubles your shirt's chest fabric, ensuring
that anything visible under your tuxedo jacket is bright white, not see-through.
There are two types of bibs: pleated (where vertical pleats run up both sides
of the button placket) and piqué (made from stiff fabric usually woven with a
dimpled pattern, and are considered more formal). Wear bib-front shirts only
with tuxedos—they don't work with more casual suits, and they'd look insane
in a boardroom.

Placket

Should you show or hide your buttons?
The decision is yours.

NO FRONT PLACKET
(FRENCH FRONT)

French front shirts don't have that folded-over and sewn strip of fabric along the buttons. Going sans placket gives your shirt a cleaner, more minimalist feel, which works for both formal or casual shirts.

FRONT PLACKET

The most common type of placket style, and one you usually can't go wrong with. Fabric is folded over and sewn with a fused interlining for a classic (and symmetrical) look.

COVERED PLACKET
(FLY FRONT)

The fly-front placket features an extra piece of fabric that covers up the buttons on your shirt. Because sometimes you've got to leave a little to the imagination.

TUXEDO FRONT
(PLAIN FRONT)

Similar to the French front, the top four buttons on this placket are removable for tuxedo studs. Please, let this style live up to its name, and wear it only with tuxes—it should never make an appearance at the office.

Cuffs

Time for a roll call.

FRENCH CUFFS

French cuffs are rolled back and held in place by cufflinks. If you're getting married or going to another event that requires a tuxedo, go for formal French cuffs. Besides, cufflinks are cool—like jewelry for your shirt.

BARREL CUFFS

Barrel cuffs don't require any rolling or cufflinks—instead, they are
secured with buttons. Most of your shirts probably have barrel cuffs.

Shoe Styles

They're the only part of a tux that isn't uniform.
Here's the lowdown on your formal footwear options.

OXFORD

Oxfords are the standard for most men's formal shoes. They come in a wide variety of styles, often embellished with toe caps, wingtips, or brogueing—offering plenty of opportunity to let your personal style shine through.

DERBY

Derby shoes look very similar to oxfords, but they are considered less formal because of their open lacing. What does that even mean? Well, the quarters (the flaps on top of the shoe that the laces are woven through) are not sewn to the vamp (basically, the top of the shoe—the part where you put your foot in), like they are on oxfords.

LOAFER

We all know what loafers look like. Slip-on, moccasin-inspired shoes, loafers were strictly casual until lawyers and businessmen started wearing them with suits in the '60s. Now loafers are considered appropriate for almost any situation, save for white tie or black tie dress codes.

SLIPPERS

Dress slippers have a much sleeker shape than the ones you loaf around in at home. They are also made from much richer materials, like velvet. Traditionally, dress slippers are considered less formal than lace-up shoes. But if we always followed tradition, then we'd probably still be practicing "marriage by capture," wearing powdered wigs, or using leeches for medical purposes. Tradition is not always best.

DRESS BOOTS

If an oxford and a work boot had a baby, that beautiful newborn would be the dress boot. It combines the best qualities of both of its parents: the masculine utility of a boot with the formal brogueing or wingtip details of an oxford. While too casual to wear with a tux, they are great to pair with most suits.

CHUKKA

Chukka boots get their funny name from their resemblance to the boots polo players wear ("chukka" is a term for a playing period in a polo game). They're versatile enough to make a great casual or dress shoe—although they are too casual to wear with a tuxedo.

CHELSEA

Chelsea boots were originally designed by Queen Elizabeth's boot maker, as casual boots for Her Majesty to wear while out walking or riding horses. The elastic strip on either side of the ankle made them easy to take on and off. Worn with a slim suit for streamlined style, they're still a no-fail look to this day.

MONK STRAP

The intermediate between the oxford and derby in terms of formality, monk straps are a similar shape, but have a buckle and strap instead of laces. If you're looking for a formal shoe option that's more eye-catching than an oxford but still works well with a tux, go for a monk strap.

HOW TO LACE

USE THE PROPER KIND OF LACE

Always use waxed cotton.

THIN ROUND LACE	THIN FLAT LACE	NYLON ATHLETIC LACE

STRAIGHTLACED OR BAR LACE

Use this traditional, formal style when lacing oxfords.

	EVEN ROWS OF EYELETS	ODD ROWS OF EYELETS

(Start with one end
of lace a little longer)

CRISS-CROSS LACING

Use with less formal shoes like brogues and derbies.

(Pull tight after lacing)

NECKTIE VS. BOW TIE

Are you a **NECKTIE** or a **BOW TIE** (PG. 140) guy? Tuxedos are almost always worn with bow ties, but you have a big choice to make when it comes to suits. *Our advice: If there's any doubt in your mind that you can pull off a bow tie with a suit, don't do it.* Half of wearing a bow tie is confidence (and it will look great if you have that confidence), and the other half is not overdoing it with the **ACCESSORIES** (PG. 142). *A classic necktie is a better choice if you're going for a subtle look.*

MATERIAL & COLOR

Silk ties are timeless and seasonless, but they aren't your only option. For summer events, cotton and linen ties in pastel colors or prints like seersucker or polka dots are classic. During winter, try a tie in wool, tweed, cashmere, or velvet. If you're doing a necktie in one of these textured winter fabrics, make sure it's skinnier in width. Anything too wide will look heavy and weigh you down.

Bow Tie Varieties

Like apple varieties, each tie has its own flavor—but they all do
the same thing.

BUTTERFLY

It's the classic bow tie shape, and it's the
most obvious go-to for any event.

BATWING

Half as tall as the classic, but what you lose
in height you gain in personality points.

DIAMOND POINT

Its asymmetrical shape makes tying more
challenging, but that's why it's so distinct.

PATTERN AND FABRIC

Shape is only the beginning. Experiment
with unique fabric patterns and textures.

HOW TO TIE A BOW TIE

Start with the bow tie lying face up. Adjust the bow tie so the right side is shorter than the left. The end on the left will be referred to as **A** and the end on the right will be referred to as **B**.

Move **A** to the right side, across **B**.

Bring **A** under **B** and up through the neck loop.

At the joint, fold **B** toward the right and then the left to create the bow shape.

Bring **A** straight down over the middle of the bow shape you made with **B**.

Fold **A** back toward the chest and pinch the fold.

Push the pinched end **A** through the loop behind **B**.

Pull on the folded parts of the bow to tighten.

Adjust until balanced on both sides.

You're done!

Waist Covering

Should you cover your waistband or not (and why should you even care about it).

CUMMERBUND

One of the guiding principles of a black tie dress code is that all the working parts of your ensemble must be covered or dressed. So the cummerbund was invented to cover up your waistband (and the awkward shirt bunching that tends to happen in that area). Cummerbunds should only be worn with tuxedos, and the material of your cummerbund should always match the material of your lapels. They're also a great place to store your phone.

LOW-CUT VEST

Get invested (sorry). Like a cummerbund, you'll usually only wear a low-cut vest— sometimes called a waistcoat—at black tie events. Low-cut vests are viewed as more formal because they have lapels (your vest lapels should match with your jacket lapels, btw), and are cut lower in the front than a typical suit vest—hence the name—to show off your shirt. Unlike the full-back vest, it is appropriate to button all buttons.

FULL-BACK VEST

All vests are not created equal. Some are backless—held in place by a single, ugly adjustable strap. If you get hot busting a move on the dance floor at that wedding reception, taking off your jacket will completely shatter the illusion of elegance you had tried so hard to maintain. Always, always go full-back vest. (And always, always leave the bottom button unbuttoned.)

BARE

If you want a more modern, effortless look, consider ditching the vest or cummerbund altogether. Going vestless is an increasingly popular, contemporary choice, and acceptable with either a tuxedo or a suit.

Cufflinks and Studs

Embellishment for your belly and regalia for your wrists.

Cufflinks and studs—unofficially known as "man jewelry"—allow some subtle personality to shine through with your formal outfit. Button studs are only for tuxedo shirts, but cufflinks are always a good choice (they don't have to be metallic, either).

Boutonnière

Get your bloom on, but only if you're getting your groom on (or you're in the wedding party).

Take this and shove it in your buttonhole: Boutonnières are an easy way to kick your panache factor up a few notches. These festive floral sprigs pinned on the suit jacket lapel are usually worn at special events like prom, or by the groom, groomsmen, and any other VIP guests at weddings. The proper way to wear a boutonnière is through the buttonhole or pinned on your left lapel, right over your heart (awww).

Pocket Square

This is not a hanky. Blow minds, not noses.

Nothing says "old-school sophistication" like a pocket square. It ties together your look, adds personality and style, and demonstrates that you're really, really good at folding things. A man wearing a pocket square is a man of confidence. Be that man.

For emergency face-drying, adhere to the time-honored mantra "one for blowin', one for showin'." Carry a hanky separately in your inner jacket pocket, and keep your pocket square tidy.

If you're going to a white-tie or black-tie event, stick to a classic white pocket square. Otherwise, the possibilities are endless. You can and should sport a colorful or patterned pocket square

pretty much any time you wear a suit jacket or blazer. Just don't commit the cardinal sin of pocket square wearing: matching it to your tie. Doing so will take your look from artfully curated to laughably contrived in no time flat.

LINEN, COTTON, OR SILK

Almost any type of fabric has pocket square potential, but most of the ones you'll find on the market are made from linen, cotton, or silk (or polyester—but we're going to leave that one out because it always looks cheap and cheesy). Cotton and linen are the most versatile, while silk has a somewhat flashier look, but by far the best drape factor. Choose whichever fabric suits you best (pun intended).

HOW TO FOLD A POCKET SQUARE

PRESIDENTIAL FOLD

This fold is best for elegant attire ranging from formal business dress to black tie.
Typically a classic white pocket square made from silk or linen is used for this fold.

ONE TIP UP FOLD

This fold suits any type of pocket square and dress code and works
with any solid colored, non-white pocket square.

PUFF FOLD

This fold suits pocket squares of any color and pattern and works best with a
sophisticated but casual-sleek outfit.

Belt and Suspenders

Options for fashionably holding up your pants.

If your tuxedo pants have belt loops on them, then they are not tuxedo pants. If you're looking for some assistance in holding up your tuxedo pants on the dance floor, then your only option is to wear suspenders—and preferably the traditional button style (also known as braces) over clip-ons.

While a tuxedo should never be worn with a belt, suits are a different story. You can wear a belt with a suit (just be sure to match your belt color to your shoes), opt for suspenders, or go without. Many men feel like their look is "unfinished" if they leave the belt loops on their pants unoccupied, but keep this in mind: your jacket will cover up the belt loops anyway, so who would know either way? If you wear a suit with a belt and no one sees it, does the belt even exist? Just a couple philosophical questions to ponder while you're deciding whether to wear a belt.

149

TUXEDOS

For the formalwear novice, the wide world of tuxedos can be perplexing. There are just so many rules, and it's really easy to end up looking like the tux is wearing you. Well, rules were (sometimes) made to be broken. It's not about the tuxedo, but about the effortless sense of style (dare we say it, swagger—ugh, cringing) that you bring to the tuxedo. If you're still feeling like you need some additional guidance, the following pages will give you plenty of no-fail outfit ideas—guaranteed to keep you looking more suave secret agent than butler or penguin.

The Black Tux
recommends combining
the following: **PEAK LAPEL TUXEDO,
WING TIP SHIRT, BLACK SATIN
DIAMOND BOW TIE, SILVER ONYX
CUFFLINKS** and **BUTTON STUDS,** and
BLACK PATENT LEATHER SHOES.

The black tux is the gold standard. It's the most formal outfit the average 21st-century man will ever wear, but that doesn't mean you should feel like a cardboard cutout. Black tuxedos are designed to highlight your personality over your outfit: the great equalizer. They're a deceptively simple way to turn heads.

BLACK TUXEDOS

FORMALITY	DRESS CODE MATCHER	SEASONALITY
	Black tie Black tie optional Creative black tie	
Stick to the basics for the biggest impact.		*Year-round, but not ideal for daytime—especially in summer.*

If you want to build your
own tuxedo look,
we recommend the following:

SHIRTS (PG. 129)

Wing tip

Pleated point
collar

Fly-front

Classic dress

SHOES (PG. 136)

Velvet slip-on

Black patent
leather

Black patent/calf
cap toe oxford

NECKWEAR (PG. 139)

Black bow tie:
*Black tie, semi-
formal,* or *black
tie optional*
events.

Black necktie:
*Black tie, semi-
formal,* or *black
tie optional*
events.

"Fun" bow tie:
Creative black tie
events.

The tux sets the foundation, but it's the details that pull it all together..

Along with a few accessories:

STUDS (PG. 144)
An optional finishing touch for tuxedo shirts.

CUFFLINKS (PG. 144)
Use cufflinks or silk knots—buttons are too casual.

BOUTONNIÈRE (PG. 145)
Only if you're the groom, or in the wedding party.

POCKET SQUARE (PG. 146)
White cotton, linen or silk are traditional. Patterns are fine, but less formal.

SUSPENDERS (PG. 148)
Dance floor insurance. For a tux, get buttons instead of clip-ons.

WAIST COVERING (PG. 142)
A matching vest, or a traditional cummerbund.

Off the cuff and on the road.

Expertly-tied bow tie? Check. Boutonnière? Check. Now just don't forget your vows.

Midnight blue is no fad: it's been around since the invention of electric lighting, which caused blue wool to appear blacker than black. Today, this tux separates you from the pack without actually breaking any rules. Midnight blue is perfect for weddings, wedding parties, and solo black tie events—not just the red carpet.

MIDNIGHT-BLUE TUXEDOS

FORMALITY	DRESS CODE MATCHER	SEASONALITY
① ② ③ **④** ⑤	Black tie Black tie optional Creative black tie	
Unexpected, but just as formal as black.		*Less stark than black in summer. Best for evenings, fall through spring.*

The Black Tux recommends combining the following: **MIDNIGHT BLUE TUXEDO, WING TIP SHIRT, BLACK SATIN DIAMOND BOW TIE, WHITE COTTON POCKET SQUARE,** and **BLACK PATENT WOOD SOLE SHOES.**

If you want to build your
own tuxedo look,
we recommend the following:

SHIRTS (PG. 129)

Wing tip

Pleated point
collar

Fly-front

Classic dress

SHOES (PG. 136)

Black patent
wood sole

Black patent
leather

Black patent/calf
cap toe oxford

NECKWEAR (PG. 139)

Black bow tie:
*Black tie, semi-
formal,* or *black
tie optional*
events.

Black necktie:
*Black tie, semi-
formal,* or *black
tie optional*
events.

"Fun" bow tie:
Creative black tie
events.

Along with a few accessories:

STUDS (PG. 144)
An optional finishing touch for tuxedo shirts.

CUFFLINKS (PG. 144)
Use cufflinks or silk knots—buttons are too casual.

BOUTONNIÈRE (PG. 145)
Only if you're the groom, or in the wedding party.

POCKET SQUARE (PG. 146)
White cotton, linen or silk are traditional. Patterns are fine, but less formal.

SUSPENDERS (PG. 148)
Dance floor insurance. For a tux, get buttons instead of clip-ons.

WAIST COVERING (PG. 142)
A matching vest, or a traditional cummerbund

A modern take on the classic—guaranteed to stand out.

Time for the finishing touches: patent shoes, bow tie, and shades.

Black tie required. Sun tan optional.

The Black Tux
recommends combining
the following: **WHITE JACKET
TUXEDO, WHITE DRESS SHIRT,
BLACK TEXTURED SILK BOW
TIE, SILVER ONYX CUFFLINKS**
and **BUTTON STUDS,** and **BLACK
PATENT LEATHER SHOES.**

All formal coats sans tails are dinner jackets, but black jackets eventually became the tuxedo and dropped the name. White dinner jackets should be ivory, which is less waiterly than true white. The old guard wore white jackets in the tropics, on cruises, and below the Mason-Dixon. Lay off this look in the snow; otherwise, though, it's okay to ignore the thermometer.

WHITE DINNER JACKETS

FORMALITY	DRESS CODE MATCHER	SEASONALITY
	Black tie Black tie optional Creative black tie	
As casual as you can get away with for black tie. Best for Optional or Creative.		*Spring through fall, or year-round in warmer climates.*

If you want to build your
own tuxedo look,
we recommend the following:

SHIRTS (PG. 129)

Wing tip

Pleated point
collar

Fly-front

Classic dress

SHOES (PG. 136)

Velvet slip-on

Black patent
leather

Black patent/calf
cap toe oxford

NECKWEAR (PG. 139)

Black bow tie:
*Black tie, semi-
formal,* or *black
tie optional*
events.

Black necktie:
*Black tie, semi-
formal,* or *black
tie optional*
events.

"Fun" bow tie:
Creative black tie
events.

Black tux for ceremony, white dinner jacket for reception. Entrance: made.

Along with a few accessories:

STUDS (PG. 144)
An optional finishing touch for tuxedo shirts.

CUFFLINKS (PG. 144)
Use cufflinks or silk knots—buttons are too casual.

BOUTONNIÈRE (PG. 145)
Only if you're the groom, or in the wedding party.

POCKET SQUARE (PG. 146)
Black or white in cotton, linen and silk are traditional. Patterns are fine, but stick to black and white.

SUSPENDERS (PG. 148)
Dance floor insurance. For dinner jackets, get buttons instead of clip-ons.

WAIST COVERING (PG. 142)
A black low cut vest or traditional cummerbund.

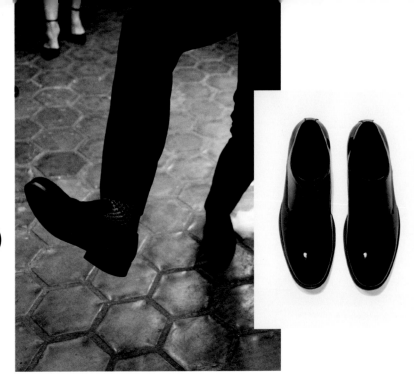

Putting on your "dancing shoes" may not magically improve your dance skills—
but at least you'll look good.

The Black Tux
recommends combining
the following: **VELVET JACKET
TUXEDO, FLY-FRONT DRESS
SHIRT, BLACK BUTTERFLY BOW
TIE, SILVER ONYX CUFFLINKS,
WHITE LINEN POCKET SQUARE**
and **CAP TOE SHOES**.

Black and midnight blue tuxedos, and white dinner jackets have proven track records of being timeless and regret-free. Still, a guy wants to stand out now and then. Substitute a jacket that challenges tradition in subtle ways, like a unique closure or fabric pattern. By unique, we do not mean camo or 10 buttons ("the Shaq"). You can even change into one of these jackets after your ceremony for your own Clark Kent/Superman moment.

MORE TUXEDO JACKETS

(VELVET, GINGHAM, AND DOUBLE-BREASTED)

FORMALITY	DRESS CODE MATCHER	SEASONALITY
① ② ③ **④** ⑤	Black tie optional Creative black tie	
Avoid for ultra-formal events.		*Year-round, though black works best fall through spring.*

If you want to build your
own tuxedo look,
we recommend the following:

SHIRTS (PG. 129)

Classic dress

Pleated point
collar

Fly-front

Pink dress

SHOES (PG. 136)

Velvet slip-on

Black patent
leather

Black patent/calf
cap toe oxford

NECKWEAR (PG. 139)

Black bow tie:
*Black tie, semi-
formal,* or *black
tie optional*
events.

Black necktie:
*Black tie, semi-
formal,* or *black
tie optional*
events.

"Fun" bow tie:
Creative black tie
events.

The Black Tux recommends combining the following: **DOUBLE-BREASTED TUXEDO, PLEATED POINT COLLAR SHIRT, BLACK SATIN DIAMOND BOW TIE, BLACK** and **WHITE CUFFLINKS, WHITE LINEN POCKET SQUARE,** and **BLACK PATENT LEATHER SHOES**.

The Black Tux
recommends combining
the following: **GINGHAM
JACKET TUXEDO, FLY-FRONT
DRESS SHIRT, BLACK SATIN
STRAIGHT BOW TIE, WHITE**
POCKET SQUARE, and **BLACK
PATENT LEATHER SHOES**.

Along with a few accessories:

STUDS (PG. 144)
For casual events, skip studs.

CUFFLINKS (PG. 144)
Cufflinks or silk knots elevate these jackets.

BOUTONNIÈRE (PG. 145)
Only if you're the groom, or in the wedding party.

POCKET SQUARE (PG. 146)
Linen or silk pair best with these jackets, but mix patterns cautiously.

SUSPENDERS (PG. 148)
Dance floor insurance. For tuxedo pants, get buttons instead of clip-ons.

WAIST COVERING (PG. 142)
A black vest, or a traditional cummerbund.

A jacket with crossover appeal—perfect for the after party.

THE SUIT
DOESN'T MAKE
THE MAN,
BUT DON'T WEAR
AN UGLY ONE

SUITS

Which suit do you wear for your wedding's season and formality level? When is it okay to wear color? And how do you accessorize the whole shebang? If you have questions about wearing a suit, congrats. You've come to the right place. Here's everything you need to know about how to look damn good on your big day.

The Black Tux
recommends combining
the following: NAVY
SUIT, WHITE DRESS
SHIRT, NAVY WOOL/
SILK TIE, SILVER PEARL
CUFFLINKS, and BROWN
LEATHER SHOES

Navy suits make anyone look authoritative, and that's a good thing when you're making lifelong promises. They don't always have to be too serious, though—navy suits are great blank slates for patterned dress shirts and interesting ties. That being said, this suit's forte is making a white dress shirt look like a laundry detergent commercial.

NAVY

FORMALITY	DRESS CODE MATCHER	SEASONALITY

① ② **③** ④ ⑤

Black tie optional
Creative black tie
Cocktail attire

Best for informal events. Can be dressed up to black-tie optional in a pinch.

Year-round, day or night.

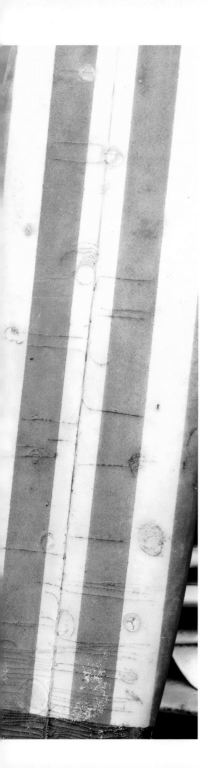

Abraham Lincoln said that you can't please all of the people all of the time, but he wasn't talking to a grey suit. You can wear medium grey year round. It's simultaneously classic and modern, low-maintenance rustic and baby-kissing stately. With its light, neutral color, it works as well outdoors as it does inside. In a word: versatile.

GREY

FORMALITY	DRESS CODE MATCHER	SEASONALITY

FORMALITY	DRESS CODE MATCHER	SEASONALITY
① ❷ ③ ④ ⑤	Cocktail attire Casual dress	🌼 🏀 🍁 ❄
Grey can strike a serious tone, but its shade is too light for formal events.		*Wear a grey suit for events spring through fall.*

The Black Tux
recommends combining
the following: **GREY SUIT,
BLUE DRESS SHIRT, SILVER
KNIT TIE, WHITE LINEN
POCKET SQUARE,** and
BROWN LEATHER SHOES

The khaki suit is the ultimate in casual-dress, warm-weather attire. Its earthy tones are perfect for outdoor weddings, and its sunny disposition makes us want to go to the state fair and gorge on corn dogs or anything fried. Visually, khaki is crisp and clean, allowing you to shake up your look with a textured tie or patterned pocket square.

KHAKI

FORMALITY	DRESS CODE MATCHER	SEASONALITY
⑤	Cocktail attire Casual dress	
Less formal than a grey suit, so keep it casual.		*Spring through fall or, in warmer climates, year-round.*

The Black Tux recommends combining the following: **KHAKI SUIT, FLY-FRONT DRESS SHIRT, SILVER KNIT TIE, BANANA LEAF POCKET SQUARE, BLACK** and **WHITE CUFFLINKS,** and **BLACK LEATHER SHOES**

The Black Tux
recommends combining
the following: **CHARCOAL SUIT,
BLUE DRESS SHIRT, NAVY SATIN
TIE, BRASS KNOT CUFFLINKS,**
and **BLACK LEATHER SHOES**

Yes, you see a lot of charcoal suits at a typical office, but that's not the whole story. Charcoal is the chameleon of suits because of its ability to adapt to its surroundings. It can be every bit as casual as a grey suit, but can quickly be outfitted for a formal event: just add a matching vest.

CHARCOAL

FORMALITY	DRESS CODE MATCHER	SEASONALITY

Black tie optional
Cocktail attire

The most casual choice for black tie optional, but best for informal events.

Year-round, day or night.

Fit Guide

For some of us, our first formalwear foray happened around age 13—a "Winter Ball," "Spring Fling," or some other cringe-inducing middle school affair full of hormonal, voice-cracking tweens. But parents of middle schoolers don't want to buy suits, so we wore our dad's: big shoulders, too-long rolled-up sleeves and all. We looked like idiots. If this near-universal cautionary tale isn't evidence of the importance of fit, what is? Don't relive the dreaded "Ill-Fitting Spring Fling Suit Incident" at your wedding. You're not 13 anymore, and your suit should reflect every bit of the cool, pulled-together man you've become (or at least pretend to be).

"YOUR BODY IS A WONDERLAND."

— JOHN MAYER

THE PERFECT FIT

Maybe you've heard that "fit is everything," but to get the right fit, you need to know where to look, and what you're looking for. Well-designed garments made with high-quality fabrics give you a leg up, forming to the shape of your body as you wear them. If the fit isn't perfect, you can solve most issues with minor tailoring or swapping the garment for a better size.

In the following pages, we'll show you how a suit should fit, and how a great fit instantly amplifies your natural style. We'll also show you how a bad fit can make you look like a schlubby, door-to-door encyclopedia salesman. Or the Incredible Hulk busting out of his street clothes. (Don't worry; just follow our cues and you won't look like either.)

A NOTE ABOUT TAILORS

A few simple alterations can make a cheap suit look great, and a great suit look like a custom piece.

SHIRT

TOO TIGHT

TOO LOOSE

JUST RIGHT

BODY

If you look like a flying squirrel, you're doing it wrong. You shouldn't see a lot of extra shirt material in the midsection unless you're a particularly muscular guy, in which case you probably have your shirts custom tailored. On the flip side, you shouldn't be able to shoot buttons at sleeve will show under the jacket sleeve—the perfect proportion to show cufflinks, if you wear them. The chart below shows how standard jacket lengths typically match with off-the-rack shirt sleeve lengths.

SHIRT SLEEVE	JACKET LENGTH
32-33	Extra Short (XS), Short (S)
34-35	Regular (R)
36-37	Long (L)
38-39	Extra Long (XL)

JUST RIGHT

✓ ··············

✓ ··············

COLLAR AND LAPELS

The jacket collar should lie flat against your dress shirt collar on the back of your neck—there shouldn't be a gap. Your lapels should also lie flat without major creases or folds. If they fly up off your chest, the jacket is probably too tight. Give your jacket some room to relax.

button. And if you can see a bit of your dress shirt under the button, your jacket is likely too tight (depending on the style). Ideally, you'll have 1 to 2 inches of space between the closed button and your abs (or the area where you wish your abs were) if you pull the fabric away from your body.

TOO TIGHT

TOO LOOSE

as one button: button it.

two buttons: only button the
never the bottom. If suit
tons: top is optional, always
dle, and never the bottom. Why
buttons if I'm not supposed to
t's like daylight saving time:
ong time ago and doesn't make
ut if you don't do it you'll
look crazy.

Body length is subjective, but ideally, the jacket body ends at your thumb knuckle when your arms are at your sides. And mind the booty: Your jacket should cover your posterior but doesn't need to drop any farther.

Jacket lengths come in Extra Short (XS), Short (S), Regular (R), Long (L), and Extra Long (XL). These sizes identify the proportional length of both the jacket sleeve and body, and correspond to your height. If you're not familiar with jacket lengths, use this chart to find the right length for your height.

Extra Short	5′
Short	5′
Regular	5′
Long	6′
Extra Long	6′

Some heights match mo
length (for example, 5′.
Choose the longer jacke
below the seat for a mo
go shorter for somethin

JUST RIGHT

Off-the-rack garments and rental suits are typically designed for the average male build. Bodybuilders, lumberjacks, and Chicagoans may find extra material in the midsection of their jackets thanks to their broad shoulders. Men with rounded stomachs, carrying more weight directly above the waist, may find the typical jacket fits their midsection but is loose in the shoulders. If you fall into one of these categories and alterations are out of the question, you may need professional guidance and creative sizing solutions to achieve a better fit. However, for a flawless and contoured fit, these body types usually require custom-made suits or major garment alterations.

TOO SHORT

TOO LONG

TOO SHORT **TOO LONG**

 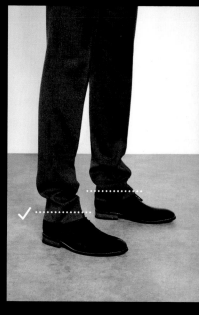

BREAK

Break is the way the front of the pant fabric folds when it sits on the top of the shoe. This is a personal style choice, but in a slim fit pant, you shouldn't be afraid to show a little sock (no break). The longest we recommend would create a small half-fold of pant fabric on the shoe, or a medium break.

Whichever fit you prefer, the pant should not end 2 inches above the ankle, nor should there be a pile of extra fabric on your shoe (we call this the Urkel/Urquelle Complex).

SUSPENDERS

LENGTH

When you pair a belt with your suit, get one in the right size. Nothing looks weirder than your belt wrapping around your waist twice. Often, your belt size is about two sizes larger than your waist size. If you are using the middle belt notch (#3 of 5), and the belt ends halfway between your fly and your hip belt loop, you have the correct size.

"MY MIND'S
TELLING ME NO.
BUT MY BODY,
MY BODY'S TELLING
ME YEAH-ESS."

— R. KELLY

Traveling with your suit is easy. By land or sea, simply hang it up in the garment bag. If you're flying, you have a choice to make: garment bag, The Black Tux box, or folded into your luggage? This really comes down to how many bags you want to bring.

GARMENT BAG

Hang everything up, secure it in the bag, and fold it in half. You can easily stow the folded bag overhead on airplanes, or politely ask your flight attendant if there's room in a closet for it to hang unfolded.

IN THE BLACK TUX BOX

We specifically designed our boxes to be perfectly sized and durable enough to protect your suit during transport. They'll fit in the overhead bins on most airplanes and have a nifty handle that makes them easy to carry. Just pack your suit into the original box that it came in, and strut onto that plane like you own it (even if you've got a middle seat in coach).

PACKED IN LUGGAGE

If you do it right, your garments will remain as wrinkle-free as they would in a garment bag—after all, it's called a suitcase. We recommend packing an important suit (think weddings) in your carry-on, just in case your checked bag is lost. Turn the page to learn how to do it.

2

Fold left shoulder
back.

Turn right shoulder inside out,
then tuck left shoulder into the right.

(4)

Fold in half lengthwise, then
fold horizontally.

Place folded jacket in center of
outstretched trousers.

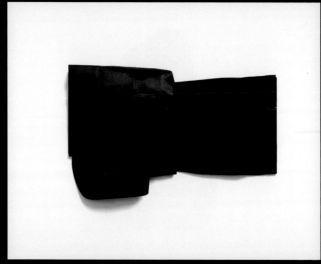

Fold trouser bottoms over jacket and
repeat with top of trousers.

❶ Index

Credits

FOUNDERS

Andrew Blackmon, Patrick Coyne

EDITORIAL

Zach Frechette, Carrie Laven, Jerod Walburn

DESIGN

Keith Scharwath, Atley Kasky, Nikka Martineau,
Everett Pelayo, Augusto Piccio IV

PRODUCT DESIGN & STYLING

Brice Pattison

PRODUCTION

Desiree Buchanan, Hank Geer, Rachel Griego,
Jessica Foitel

ILLUSTRATION

Cynthia Kittler

PHOTOGRAPHY

The Collaborationist, Logan Cole, Dimitri Newman,
Carlos Rios

ICONS

Mikey Burton

COPY EDITING

Paige Worthy

INDEXING

Fred Leise

SPECIAL THANKS

Jacob Acosta, Cameron Bell, Debi Bergerson, Lauren Boortz,
Caroline Buenrostro, Sarah Danley, Kevin Diamond,
Grazi DiPaolo, Mike Gammarino, Matt Gierl, Lara Kapelke,
John Mitchell, Erin Neff, James Paulson, Mariko Traina,
Whitney Wyckoff, Sarah Yang, Derek Zornizer

DOVETAIL

Published by Dovetail Press in Brooklyn, New York, a division of Assembly Brands LLC.

For details or ordering information, contact the publisher at the address below or email info@dovetail.press.

Dovetail Press
42 West Street #403
Brooklyn, NY 11222
www.dovetail.press

Library of Congress Cataloging-in-Publication data is on file with the publisher.

ISBN: 978-0-9987399-9-1

Second Edition

Printed in China

10 9 8 7 6 5 4 3 2